Langenscheidts

Grundwortschatz Englisch

Übungsbuch

Völlige Neuentwicklung

von
Sonia Brough

Herausgegeben von
der Langenscheidt-Redaktion

Langenscheidt

Berlin · München · Wien · Zürich · New York

Autorin: Dr. Sonia Brough
Redaktion: Thomas Bennett-Long
Layout: Josef Krapf, Helmut Fischer
Illustrationen: Matthias Weis

Auflage:	*5.*	*4.*	*3.*	*2.*	*1.*	*Letzte Zahlen*
Jahr:	*2004*	*03*	*02*	*01*	*00*	*maßgeblich*

Druck: Clausen & Bosse
*Printed in Germany · ISBN 3-468-**20126-**5*

VORWORT

Wozu dient dieses Übungsbuch?

Mit diesem Arbeitsbuch zu *Langenscheidts Grundwortschatz Englisch* möchten wir Ihnen die Gelegenheit geben, Ihren englischen Wortschatz systematisch und effektiv zu festigen und zu erweitern.

Dazu bieten sich die mehr als 300 Vokabeltests in diesem Band bestens an. Die abwechslungsreiche Auswahl an Übungen reicht von Einsetz- und Zuordnungsübungen über Multiple-Choice-Fragen und Aussprachetests bis hin zu Buchstabenspielen. Somit wird das Vokabellernen nicht zur sturen „Paukerei“, sondern macht auch Spaß.

Wie im *Grundwortschatz Englisch* werden die Vokabeln auch in diesem Übungsband in Sinnzusammenhängen präsentiert, damit man sie sich besser einprägen kann. Es werden dabei auch besonders die Problemfälle im englischen Wortschatz berücksichtigt. Heißt z. B. „Straße“ auf Englisch „road“ oder „street“? Wann sagt man für „borgen“ „to borrow“, wann „to lend“? Auch wortschatzbezogene Aspekte der Grammatik werden geübt, zum Beispiel der Gebrauch des Artikels „the“ mit bestimmten Substantiven wie etwa „life“ und „death“, oder der unterschiedliche Gebrauch von „for“ und „since“ als Übersetzung von „seit“.

Wie ist das Buch aufgebaut?

In seinem Aufbau folgt dieses Übungsbuch dem erfolgreichen System von *Langenscheidts Grundwortschatz Englisch.* Selbstverständlich kann das Übungsbuch aber auch ohne Grundwortschatz benutzt werden. Die Nummerierung der Abschnitte entspricht genau der des Grundwortschatzes. Die Übungen in jedem Abschnitt sind entweder nach den zwei Wichtigkeitsstufen 1–2000 und 2001–4000 unterteilt oder sie verbinden beide Stufen (als 1–4000 gekennzeichnet), um ausführlichere Tests anbieten zu können.

Für wen ist das Buch gedacht?

Der Übungsband ist für alle gedacht, die ihren englischen Wortschatz festigen und erweitern wollen. Er eignet sich für die Schule, für das Studium, für die Erwachsenenbildung, für die Arbeit, für das Surfen im Internet, für den Urlaub, für

Geschäftsreisen: kurz, für alle Situationen, in denen Sie Ihr Englisch aktiv oder passiv anwenden möchten. Die Übungen sind sowohl zum Lernen als auch zur Auffrischung von Vokabular gedacht.

Wie benutze ich das Übungsbuch?

Sie müssen das Buch nicht systematisch von A bis Z durcharbeiten, sondern Sie können sich ruhig die Sachgebiete aussuchen, die für Sie besonders wichtig sind.

- Bevor Sie sich mit einem Themenbereich beschäftigen, können Sie Ihren Wortschatz mit dem entsprechenden Abschnitt aus *Langenscheidts Grundwortschatz Englisch* (Bestellnr. 20122) auffrischen.
- Versuchen Sie, die Übung bzw. Übungen zu dem gewählten Thema auszuführen und vergleichen Sie dann Ihre Antworten mit denen im Schlüssel am Ende des Buchs. Wenn Sie bestimmte Fragen nicht bzw. nicht richtig beantwortet haben, können Sie die entsprechenden Vokabeln zum Beispiel auf Karteikarten notieren, auf denen Sie das englische Wort auf der Vorderseite aufschreiben und die deutsche Bedeutung auf der Rückseite.
- Nachdem Sie sich diese unbekannten Vokabeln fest „einverleibt“ haben, wiederholen Sie die Übung(en). Um zu testen, ob die Wörter nun auch richtig „sitzen“, empfiehlt es sich, die Übung(en) nach ein paar Tagen noch einmal zu wiederholen. Haken Sie dann im Übungsbuch die Fragen ab, die Sie richtig beantwortet haben, und konzentrieren Sie sich auf die Vokabeln, die Sie noch nicht beherrschen. Diese Schritte sollten wiederholt werden, bis Sie alle Vokabeln sicher beherrschen.

Wichtig ist dabei, dass Sie sich nicht zuviel auf einmal vornehmen. Besser jeden Tag ein wenig (etwa 1 bis 2 Abschnitte, z. B. Körper bzw. Körper und Aussehen), als eine „Mammutsitzung“ am Wochenende. So lernen Sie Ihren englischen Wortschatz am effektivsten und werden ihn sicher anwenden können.

Wir wünschen Ihnen dabei viel Spaß und Erfolg!

Autorin und Verlag

INHALT

THEMENBEZOGENE BEGRIFFE 1

Der Mensch 1.1

Körper und Wesen 1.1.1

Körper 1.1.1.1

1–2000

1. Wie heißen die verschiedenen Körperteile?

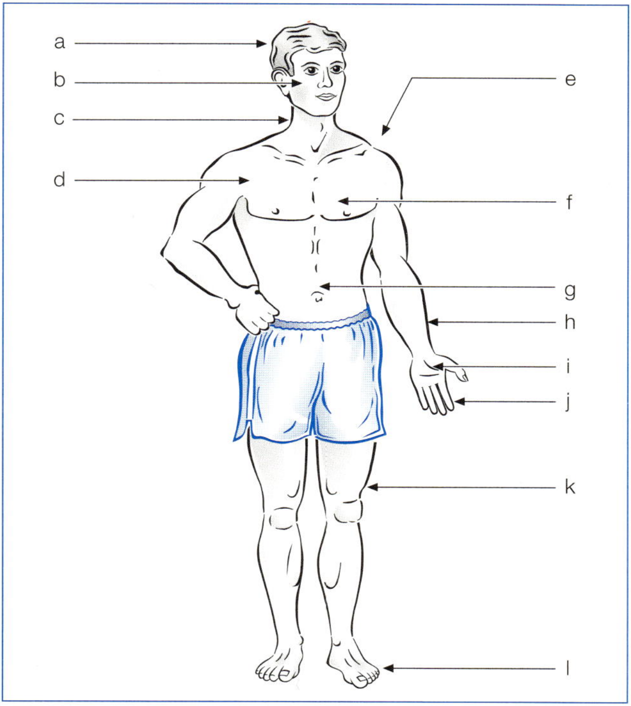

a) ....
b) ....
c) ....
d) ....
e) ....
f) ....
g) ....
h) ....
i) ....
j) ....
k) ....
l) ....

2. Wie heißen die Teile des Gesichts?

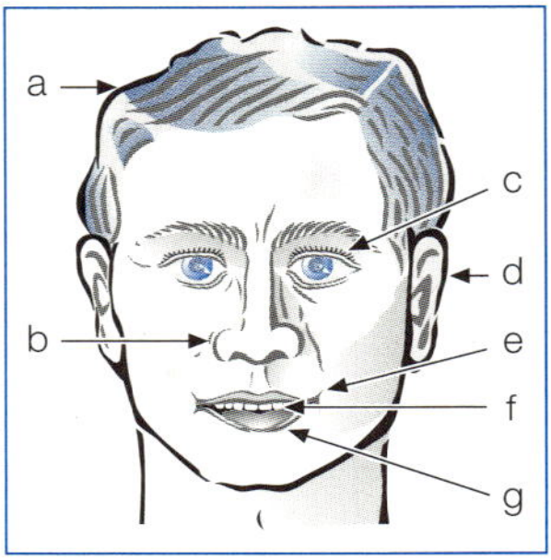

a) ....
b) ....
c) ....
d) ....
e) ....
f) ....
g) ....

2001–4000

3. Ordnen Sie die folgenden Körperteile der richtigen Reihenfolge nach, von oben nach unten.

ankle thumb shoulder elbow
lip wrist cheek
toe forehead knee

a) ....
b) ....
c) ....
d) ....
e) ....
f) ....
g) ....
h) ....
i) ....
j) ....

4. Füllen Sie die Lücken mit den Wörtern aus dem Kasten.

heel bone cheek breath skin
sweat muscle chin breast
waist fist joint brain
flesh nerve breathe limb

a) He's very strong – he's got big ....s.
b) Think! Use your ....!
c) I never use a deodorant – I don't ....

d) He has very fair, sensitive .... just like his mother.
e) My grandmother's got a double .... – it wobbles when she talks.
f) Take a deep .... Now .... normally again.
g) Jeremy broke a few ....s in his skiing accident.
h) Her .... looks swollen because she's got a big sweet in her mouth.
i) Not many mothers .... -feed their babies these days.
j) I need a bigger belt. I must have put on weight around my ....
k) The teacher banged the table with her ....
l) Our neighbours are so noisy – they really get on our ....s.
m) I always get pains in my elbows, knees and other ....s in cold weather.
n) Arms and legs are known as ....s.
o) He cut his finger badly with the bread knife, but fortunately it was only a .... wound.
p) I can balance on my toes, but if I try to balance on my ....s I usually fall backwards.

Aussehen 1.1.1.2

1–4000

1. Fügen Sie das Adjektiv mit der gegenteiligen Bedeutung vom unterstrichenen Wort ein.

a) He's fat, but his brother is ....
b) He's short, but his brother is ....
c) He's ...., but his brother is very good-looking.
d) He has very small eyes, but his brother has lovely .... eyes.

2. Welche Beschreibung passt zu welchem Bild? Fügen Sie die Buchstaben ein.

pretty face .....
long beard .....
blond curls .....
handsome young man .....

3. Haken Sie die zwei Adjektive ab, die jeweils passen.

a) Your father is very
- ☐ handsome.
- ☐ beautiful.
- ☐ good-looking.

b) My sister is quite
- ☐ pretty.
- ☐ attractive.
- ☐ handsome.

c) What a
- ☐ pretty
- ☐ beautiful
- ☐ good-looking baby!

d) I think your twin brother is
- ☐ attractive.
- ☐ pretty.
- ☐ good-looking.

Geist und Verstand

1.1.1.3

1–4000

1. Wie lauten die Adjektive zu diesen Substantiven? Z. B. *happiness – happy*.

a) intelligence ....
b) reason ....
c) wisdom ....
d) sense ....
e) skill ....

2. Unterstreichen Sie das Verb, das im Satz jeweils passt.

a) I can't *remember/realize* where the car keys are.
b) I *thought/considered* he was your teacher.
c) Do you *imagine/understand* what I mean?
d) She has to work so hard that she's *thinking of/imagining* changing her job.
e) We didn't *see/realize* you were so much older than us.

3. Füllen Sie die Lücken mit den Wörtern aus dem Kasten.

mind	skill	imagination	wise	remember
keen	impression	fool	sensible	mad
memory	stupid	interested	understand	idea

Meet the class

Our teacher is Mrs Pinkerton. She is very old and .... and knows a lot about life. She also has a good ....: she can .... teaching my grandfather about fifty years ago and says he always got good marks for his schoolwork. He was very clever, not .... like me. Well, I may not be very intelligent, but I have a lot of other ....s, such as being able to play football and computer games. My favourite classmate is Robert. He isn't very .... in school, but he writes good essays because he has a lively .... Penny is the prettiest girl in class, but unfortunately she isn't very .... on boys yet. Frank is the teacher's pet: he's well-behaved and full of clever ....s. Then there's Raymond, the classroom

.... He's always doing crazy things and he drives Mrs Pinkerton .... with his practical jokes and silly behaviour. When she tells him off, he pretends he can't .... her. Well, those are just a few of the people in my class to give you a first .... Mrs Pinkerton is very kind to us all – she says she is fascinated by young ....s and believes that with her help we will all turn into .... adults one day. She's very optimistic.

1.1.1.4 Charakter

1–4000

1. Wie lautet das passende Adjektiv?

careless funny proud charming
generous serious shy honest
lazy rude fair polite cruel

a) Helen never laughs. She's very ....
b) Barney kicks his cat. He's ....
c) Sam says he never lies. He says he is totally ....
d) Lucy keeps knocking things over. She's ....
e) His parents taught him good manners, that's why he's so ....
f) Mr Parks treats us all equally. He's very ....
g) Jim makes us all laugh. He's so ....
h) Andrew always shares his sweets. He's very ....
i) Rupert knows how to treat girls. He's quite ....
j) Sarah never helps in the house. She's ....
k) Peter came top of the class and he's very .... of the fact.
l) He came in and didn't even say hello. He's so ....
m) Susan never talks to anyone. She's very ....

2. Wie lautet das Gegenteil von diesen Adjektiven?

a) rude ....
b) honest ....
c) serious ....
d) careful ....
e) patient ....
f) good ....
g) fair ....
h) faithful ....

3. Welches Wort passt jeweils nicht? Streichen Sie es durch.

a) I admire your *pride/courage/patience.*
b) He's always been *faithful/good/curious* to his wife.
c) It takes a lot of *quality/courage/character* to do that.
d) My mother's got a great sense of *patience/humour/pride.*

4. Füllen Sie die Lücken mit den Wörtern aus dem Kasten.

generous	polite	coward
courage	friendly	

a) Trevor isn't very brave. In fact, he's a real ....
b) Sheila's being extremely brave about her brain operation. She's got a lot of ....
c) I always open the door for ladies. I think I'm very ....
d) My grandfather isn't at all stingy. In fact, he's quite ....
e) He seems to be quite .... – he always says hello in the street.

Fühlen und Empfinden 1.1.1.5

1–4000

1. Welche Adjektive passen in welche Spalte?

delighted	angry	unhappy	glad
sad	happy	upset	
excited	jealous	disappointed	

☺	☹
....	....
....	....
....	....
....	....
	....
	....

2. Welche Präposition fehlt jeweils?

a) I'm sorry .... last night.
b) He fell in love .... his cousin.
c) Have you ever been .... love?
d) I'm tired .... doing all your homework for you.
e) You should be ashamed .... your behaviour.
f) We were shocked .... the news.
g) There's no need to be afraid .... the dogs.
h) I long .... a holiday somewhere far away.
i) The teacher was mad .... us for forgetting our sports kit.

3. Wie lautet das Gegenteil?

a) love ....
b) despair ....
c) happy ....
d) pleasant ....
e) satisfied ....
f) exciting ....

4. Wie lauten die fehlenden Worte? Der erste Buchstabe ist als Hilfe angegeben. Setzen Sie die Verben in die richtige Zeitform.

fall hope pleasant nervous like
feeling lonely long fun delighted
sensitive surprised feel happy exciting

Matchmaking

Joan wanted to introduce Cathy to her older brother Michael and arranged for them to meet in a nearby café. Cathy was 15 and felt quite n.......... about meeting him. She was an only child and had had quite a l.......... childhood. She was shy and didn't have many friends. Now she l.......... for a boyfriend. Well, Michael turned out to be a very s....... young man who l.......... quiet girls with a sense of humour. They spent two p.......... hours talking and laughing together in the café and then went on to a disco, where they had great f.......... dancing until after midnight.
The next morning Cathy was s.......... but d.......... to receive a phone call from Michael. He said that he f.......... so h.......... after the last evening and that he h.......... they could meet again very soon. Cathy shared

these f.........s. In fact, she had f.......... in love with Michael at first sight. They agreed to meet in the café again that afternoon. It was to be the start of a very e.......... romance, thanks to Joan's clever matchmaking.

5. Welches Wort aus dem Kasten passt jeweils?

sympathy	pleasure	love	shock	fear

a) .... – of music; – at first sight; – for one's parents
b) .... – of spiders; – of flying; – of failure
c) .... – at the news; in a state of –; get a –
d) .... – for the victims; express one's –; letter of –
e) .... give –; bring someone –; it was my –

Gesundheit und Krankheit 1.1.1.6

1–2000

1. Füllen Sie die Lücken mit den Wörtern aus dem Kasten.

cough	headache	sick (2x)	pain	flu
cold	health	temperature		
well	hurt	ill	accident	

a) Ron feels very hot. I think he's got a ....
b) – Does your head hurt?
– Yes, I've had a bad .... since yesterday.
c) The .... happened because he was driving too fast.
d) My nose is running – I hope I'm not getting a ...., or even ....
e) We wish the bride and groom .... and happiness.
f) – How are you feeling?
– Not very ....

g) This is the new hospital for .... children.
h) He has been complaining about ....s in his chest.
i) Does it .... when I do that?
j) He's never been seriously .... in his life.
k) This flight is so bumpy – I feel ....
l) My chest hurts every time I ....

2001–4000

2. Was fehlt ihnen? Vervollständigen Sie jeweils den Satz.

a) He's ....
b) He's got ....
c) She's got an
....
....
d) She's got a
....
....
e) She's ....
f) His finger is ....

3. Welches Verb aus dem Kasten fehlt jeweils? Setzen Sie es – wo nötig – in die richtige Zeitform.

injure	faint	tremble	heal
swell	recover	break down	

a) When she heard the news, she began to .... all over.
b) Three soldiers .... in the heat.
c) When his wife left him, he .... completely.
d) He .... very quickly from the accident, but he still has a few cuts and bruises which will take some time to ....
e) How many people were .... in the coach crash?
f) If I sit for too long, my feet start to ....

Leben und Tod 1.1.1.7

1–4000

1. Welche Wörter aus dem Kasten passen in welche Spalte?

fatal	birth	alive	funeral
kill	survive	exist	die
born	bury	grow up	dead body

life	*death*
....	....
....	....
....	....
....	....
....	....
....	....

2. Wie lauten die Substantive?

a) live ....
b) die ....
c) young ....
d) exist ....
e) born ....

3. Bringen Sie diese Ausdrücke in die richtige zeitliche Reihenfolge.

death, old age, childhood, birth, youth

....

4. *Life, live* oder *alive*? Füllen Sie die Lücken.

a) Do you really believe there's .... in outer space?
b) Nobody .... s forever.
c) Thousands of .... s were lost in the earthquake.
d) After surviving that car accident, I'm so happy to be .... From now on I'm going to .... to the full.

5. *Die, dead* oder *death*? Füllen Sie die Lücken und setzen Sie das Verb *die* in die richtige Zeitform.

a) It was hard to tell whether he was .... or alive.
b) She didn't know how to tell the children that their grandfather had ....
c) .... is something we find difficult to understand.
d) She .... a peaceful .... with all her family around her.

6. Mit oder ohne *the*? Übersetzen Sie diese Sätze.

a) Das Leben ist gut.

....

b) Das Leben der Eskimos ist hart.

....

c) Der Tod ist schwer zu verstehen.

....

d) Der Tod der drei Studenten war ein Schock.

....

Aktivitäten 1.1.2

Wachen und Schlafen 1.1.2.1

1–4000

1. Ergänzen Sie diesen Dialog mit den Wörtern aus dem Kasten. Setzen Sie die Verben – wo nötig – in die richtige Zeitform.

sleep	asleep	awake	wake up
dream	tired	fall	
bed	go	dream	get

Jack: I'm . . . . I think I'll go to . . . .
Roger: Do you need a lot of . . . . ?
Jack: Only about ten hours a night.
Roger: How long does it take you to . . . . to sleep?
Jack: A few seconds.
Roger: And when you're . . . . do you . . . . ?
Jack: Yes, I have very pleasant . . . . s – about sleeping.
Roger: Hmm. What time do you usually . . . . up in the mornings?
Jack: As soon as I . . . .
Roger: And when you're . . . . do you feel rested?
Jack: Zzzzzzz...
Roger: Oh dear, I think he's . . . . asleep.

Sinneswahrnehmungen 1.1.2.2

1–4000

1. Fügen Sie das fehlende Verb ein. In manchen Fällen sind zwei möglich.

a) You . . . . with your eyes.
b) You . . . . with your ears.
c) You . . . . with your hands.
d) You . . . . with your tongue.
e) You . . . . with your nose.

2. Wie lautet das fehlende Wort?

Taste, smell and touch are three of the five . . . .

3. *See, look, watch, hear* oder *listen*? Füllen Sie die Lücken.

Colin: Did you . . . . Inspector Morse on television last night?
Terry: No, I never . . . . TV. I prefer to . . . . to the radio.
Colin: So did you . . . . the Oasis concert from Dublin?
Terry: No, I just spent a quiet evening . . . . ing at my holiday photos.
Colin: Could I . . . . them some time?
Terry: Not for a while. I'm going to be busy in the evenings for the next few months . . . . ing and . . . . ing to the Prom concerts from the Albert Hall on TV and radio.

1.1.2.3 Körperpflege

1–4000

1. Versuchen Sie, die zehn in diesem Quadrat versteckten Gegenstände aus dem Badezimmer aufzufinden, indem Sie von oben nach unten und von links nach rechts lesen.

g	f	t	a	d	h	i	e	f	s
s	p	o	w	d	e	r	s	b	o
c	d	o	i	r	e	t	h	t	u
x	i	t	u	d	n	c	o	m	b
k	c	h	a	o	n	l	w	a	r
b	k	p	s	t	b	x	e	k	w
i	r	a	z	o	r	r	r	e	t
t	t	s	t	w	u	l	o	u	l
b	a	t	h	e	s	o	a	p	q
u	w	e	q	l	h	s	a	m	g

Tätigkeiten 1.1.2.4

1–2000

1. *Make* oder *do*? Setzen Sie – wo nötig – das Verb in die richtige Zeitform.

a) Mum, I've .... my homework. Can I go out now?
b) I spent hours .... this cake for Roger's birthday party.
c) Do you always have to .... such a noise when you're playing with your dolls?
d) – Have you .... your room yet?
– No, I've only .... the bed. I haven't .... the hoovering or dusting.
e) You've .... a lot of mistakes in your English essay. I'm afraid you'll have to .... it again.
f) Shall I .... some tea while you .... the shopping?
g) Aunt Flora has .... me a lovely dress for the dance, but I need someone to .... my hair.

2. ARBEIT = *job? / work?* Übersetzen Sie die folgenden Sätze.

a) Er geht von Montag bis Donnerstag in die Arbeit.
....
b) Gefällt dir deine neue Arbeit?
....
c) Das war eine schlechte Arbeit.
....
d) Die Arbeit fängt um neun an.
....

1–4000

3. Welches Verb aus dem Kasten passt jeweils?

act plan prepare
manage make decide
practise try work do

a) .... – for a test; – for war; – dinner
b) .... – on Sundays; – as a childminder; – hard
c) .... – singing; – the piano; – regularly

d)	....	– to study; – against something; – what to do
e)	....	– to improve; – again; – hard
f)	....	– strangely; – quickly; – like a fool
g)	....	– to get rich; – to survive; – it
h)	....	– a holiday; – ahead; – to emigrate
i)	....	– a mess; – money; – breakfast
j)	....	– nothing; – the washing-up; – some work

4. Zu welchen dieser Verben gehört ein gleichlautendes Substantiv? Unterstreichen Sie sie.

a) plan	b) act	c) attempt	d) manage
e) work	f) intend	g) prepare	h) try

1.1.2.5 Umgang mit Dingen

1–2000

1. Zu welchem Verb passen diese Substantive? Ordnen Sie sie in die entsprechenden Spalten. Manche Wörter passen in mehrere Spalten.

fish	fist	door	train
finger	fridge	medicine	bread
tree	book	ball	chin
head	hair	window	mouse

open	*cut*	*shake*	*catch*
....	....	....	....
....	....	....	....
....	....	....	....
....	....	....	....
....	....	....	
	....	....	

1–4000

2. Was tun sie? Vervollständigen Sie die Sätze.

a) He's .... the button. (*drückt auf*)
b) She's .... the towel. (*reißt*)
c) He's .... for his tennis racket. (*sucht*)
d) She's .... the door. (*streicht ... an*)
e) He's .... the baby's nappies. (*wechselt*)
f) She's .... at the door. (*klopft*)

3. Wie lautet das Gegenteil?

a) fold ....
b) turn off ....
c) lose ....
d) fill ....
e) hit ....
f) save ....
g) bend ....
h) close ....
i) connect ....
j) wrap ....
k) catch ....

4. Wie lauten die Vergangenheitsformen?
Z. B. *bend bent bent*

a) hold ....
b) use ....
c) burn ....
d) wind ....
e) press ....
f) dig ....
g) find ....
h) spoil ....
i) saw ....
j) rub ....
k) hang ....
l) catch ....
m) light ....
n) split ....
o) shut ....
p) keep ....
q) tear ....
r) cut ....

Bewegen von Gegenständen 1.1.2.6

1–4000

1. Welches Verb aus dem Kasten passt jeweils?

drag	put	push	pull	remove
lift	pick up	send	raise	
lower	lay	turn	carry	load

a) .... – the door open; – a bicycle; – someone over; – hard

b) .... – a handbag; – a case; – a baby

c) .... – a car up; – a truck; – furniture into a van; – cases into the boot

d) .... – one's hand; – a platform to a higher level; – one's eyebrows

e) .... – a letter; – a message; – a package by courier

f) .... – a baby on the bed; – flowers on a grave; – a parquet floor

g) .... – pieces of glass; – rubbish; – a handkerchief somebody has dropped

h) .... – a load; – a chair; – a sack

i) .... – a cord; – a case on wheels; – a door shut

j) .... – some tissues in one's pocket; – a child to bed; – money into the bank

k) .... – a key; – a car round; – a tap off

l) .... – a child along; – one's feet; – a chair onto the balcony

m) .... – a name from a list; – dirt; – some books from the library

n) .... – a flag; – one's eyes; – a rope from the roof

2. BRINGEN = *take?/bring?*

Übersetzen Sie die folgenden Sätze. Setzen Sie die passende Verbform ein.

a) Bring den Hund zurück zu deinem Freund.

....

b) Was hast du ins Haus gebracht?

....

c) Peter hat ihn zu seinem Onkel gebracht.

....

d) Könntest du mir meine Tabletten bringen?

....

Geben und Nehmen

1.1.2.7

THEMEN

1–4000

1. Entwirren Sie die unterstrichenen Wörter und übersetzen Sie sie anschließend.

a) I'm not allowed to <u>cepact</u> any gifts.
.... *Übersetzung:* ....

b) You can <u>peke</u> the change.
.... *Übersetzung:* ....

c) We're going to <u>plist</u> the profit.
.... *Übersetzung:* ....

d) Could you <u>assp</u> me the salt, please?
.... *Übersetzung:* ....

e) My mother told me never to <u>robwor</u> money from friends.
.... *Übersetzung:* ....

f) My father told me never to <u>deln</u> money to relatives.
.... *Übersetzung:* ....

g) Where did you <u>teg</u> that lovely shirt?
.... *Übersetzung:* ....

h) <u>veig</u> it back to me!
.... *Übersetzung:* ....

i) We <u>harse</u> a babysitter.
.... *Übersetzung:* ....

j) The demonstrators say they are going to <u>cupyco</u> the government building.
.... *Übersetzung:* ....

k) Please don't <u>valee</u> me on my own!
.... *Übersetzung:* ....

l) Did you <u>versere</u> a table?
.... *Übersetzung:* ....

m) He didn't <u>trunre</u> the dog to its owner for three days.
.... *Übersetzung:* ....

n) Please <u>eakt</u> the cake home with you.
.... *Übersetzung:* ....

o) He should <u>vericee</u> the letter by Monday.
.... *Übersetzung:* ....

2. BORGEN = *borrow?/lend?*

Welche Übersetzung stimmt jeweils? Unterstreichen Sie sie.

Mr Jones:	Who did you *borrow/lend* the money from?
Carol:	David *borrowed/lent* it to me.
Mr Jones:	I've told you never to *borrow/lend* money.
Carol:	But David was happy to *borrow/lend* me it. He only charges 20 % interest a month.

1.1.3 *Lernen und Wissen*

1–2000

1. Welches Verb aus dem Kasten passt jeweils?

read	write	learn	know

a) .... – vocabulary; – a language; – to type; – to drive; – how to use a computer; – fast
b) .... – poetry; – a letter; – in ink; – home; – for a newspaper; – a book
c) .... – some Greek; – a lot about history; – all the kings and queens of England
d) .... – a story; – a letter; – fast; – in bed; – a file; – in front of the class

2001–4000

2. Wie lautet die passende Präposition?

a) It's a poem .... life in the city.
b) She always writes notes .... the margins of the books she reads.
c) I described the woman .... the policeman.
d) Mum, could you test me .... my irregular verbs?
e) Her knowledge .... flowers is very good.
f) The crater was created .... a meteor.
g) I don't like doing experiments .... dead frogs.
h) For this job you need an ability .... think fast.

3. Unterstreichen Sie das Verb, das passt.

a) Who *discovered/invented* the steam engine?
b) Many people believe that God *created/discovered* the universe.
c) I have plenty of *experience/practice* with difficult children.
d) We did a lot of chemical *experiences/experiments* at school.
e) I don't think that he has the *ability/practice* to become a musician.
f) It's a big dictionary – it has four *texts/volumes.*

1–4000

4. Welches Wort aus dem Kasten passt zur jeweiligen Definition?

ink	pages	notebook	volumes
type	letters	writer	novel
library	test	poems	expert

a) A place where you keep books: ....
b) Something you make notes in: ....
c) A poet writes these: ....
d) A long fictional story in book form: ....
e) To write using a keyboard: ....
f) The alphabet has 26 of them: ....
g) You turn them over in a book: ....
h) Another word for a specialist: ....
i) You find this in a pen: ....
j) You can pass or fail it: ....
k) Another word for author: ....
l) An encyclopaedia usually consists of several of these: ....

5. LERNEN = *learn?/study?*

Welche Übersetzung stimmt jeweils? Unterstreichen Sie sie.

a) Peter can't come out – he's *learning/studying* for his English exam.
b) It took me hours to *learn/study* the poem by heart.
c) She says she wants to *learn/study* history at Durham University.

d) I've *learnt/studied* a lot of new English vocabulary today.
e) My father *learnt/studied* to speak Japanese in two years.

1.1.4 *Verhalten*

1.1.4.1 Allgemeines Verhalten

1–2000

1. Welche Dialoghälften aus der linken und rechten Spalte passen jeweils zusammen?

a) Why are you smiling?

b) I've forgotten when he said he would leave.

c) Will we have to wait long?

d) We were expecting you earlier.

e) Were you able to watch Billy Connolly?

f) Who's taking care of the children?

u) That's because you weren't paying attention.

v) It depends on how urgent the matter is.

w) Yes, we laughed till we cried.

x) Well, I think it's the father's duty in this case.

y) I'm sorry, but I just didn't notice the time.

z) That's none of your business.

a) .... c) .... e) ....
b) .... d) .... f) ....

2001–4000

2. Füllen Sie die Lücken mit den Wörtern aus dem Kasten.

charge	stand	affairs	manners
habits	memories	effort	
miss	way	look after	

Alf: She doesn't know how to behave – she hasn't got any .... at all. She smokes and drinks. In fact, she's got lots of bad .... She makes no ....

to do any work in the house, and you should see the .... she treats me – as if she was in .... of the place. I can't .... it any more. I really .... my parents – they used to .... me properly. Ah, the .... of a happy family life back home in Dorset!

Dick: Then why don't you leave her and go back to your mum and dad?

Alf: Why don't you keep your nose out of my private ....!

3. Welches Verb aus der linken Spalte verbindet man am ehesten mit welchem Substantiv in der rechten Spalte?

a) watch	u) courage
b) stand	v) money
c) dare	w) eyes
d) look after	x) pain
e) behave	y) appearance
f) neglect	z) manners

a)	c)	e) ....
b)	d)	f) ....

Verhalten gegen Menschen 1.1.4.2

1–2000

1. Versuchen Sie, die unterstrichenen Wörter zu entwirren.

a) – Paul's very <u>linets</u> (..........).
– Ssshhh! Don't <u>bustird</u> (..........) him – he's meditating.

b) There's no <u>cuxese</u> (..........) for it. He should have <u>plehed</u> (..........) her out in that difficult situation.

c) I <u>rimpose</u> (..........) to do everything in my <u>woper</u> (..........) to get him the job.

d) <u>minder</u> (..........) me what your name is again.

e) <u>A dink</u> (..........) old gentleman offered to <u>leph</u> (..........) me off the bus with the baby.

2001–4000

2. Fügen Sie die fehlenden Präfixe ein (jeweils 2–3 Buchstaben).

a) He's always trying to .... press the girls.
b) I try to .... courage the children to read books instead of playing computer games.
c) She doesn't have much .... fidence, but she's doing well at school.
d) I'll never .... give you for what you did.
e) They will be .... sulted if you don't eat it.
f) Your friends are a bad .... fluence on you.
g) Can't you .... suade him to get a haircut?
h) Could you explain that again? I'm .... fused.
i) Remember, you are .... presenting your country at the tournament.

3. Ersetzen Sie die unterstrichenen Wörter jeweils mit einem aus dem Kasten, das eine ähnliche Bedeutung hat.

convince	curse	confidence
brag	fighting	fight
lead	upset	copy

a) It was a long, hard <u>struggle</u>. ....
b) Where did you learn to <u>swear</u> like that? ....
c) We had to <u>guide</u> the whole class through the museum. ....
d) I can't <u>persuade</u> her that she's wrong. ....
e) The twins just won't stop <u>quarrelling</u>. ....
f) I always manage to <u>offend</u> my mother-in-law. ....
g) He likes to <u>boast</u> about how many cars he's got. ....
h) He has no originality. He has to <u>imitate</u> other artists. ....
i) She says she has no <u>trust</u> in politicians. ....

1–4000

4. Ersetzen Sie die unterstrichenen Ausdrücke durch ihr Gegenteil. Der erste Buchstabe ist als Hilfe angegeben.

a) He never <u>tells the truth</u>. l . . . .
b) Don't <u>discourage</u> him. e . . . .
c) Why are you trying to <u>blame</u> her? e . . . .
d) That was a very <u>kind</u> thing to say. u . . . .
e) My mother can't stand the <u>silence</u> in her new flat. n . . . .

5. Womit reimt es sich? Unterstreichen Sie das richtige Wort.

a) threat:	street	bet
b) cheat:	street	bet
c) damn:	ham	pan
d) swear:	pair	steer
e) power:	lower	shower
f) kind:	sinned	find
g) guide:	lead	hide

Sprache und Sprechabsichten 1.1.5

Sprache 1.1.5.1

1–2000

1. *Talk, speak, say* oder *tell*? Setzen Sie die Verben in die richtige Zeitform.

a) – James is moving to Ireland.
– Who . . . . you that?
– Polly . . . . so.
b) Mary isn't . . . . to me any more because I . . . . everyone that she was getting divorced.
c) Do you . . . . any foreign languages?
d) I . . . . you not to eat unwashed fruit.
e) Last night Dad . . . . that I should move into my own flat.
f) Our children don't lie. We have brought them up to . . . . the truth.

1–4000

2. Fügen Sie jeweils das fehlende Wort aus dem Kasten ein.

crying shouting whispering
conversation discussion argument

a) She's .... in his ear.
b) He's .... at the dog.
c) The baby's ....
d) They're having a .... about politics.
e) They're having an ....
f) He's in the middle of a telephone ....

3. Wie lautet das Substantiv?

a) spell ....
b) express ....
c) pronounce ....
d) discuss ....
e) speak ....

4. Welches Substantiv aus dem Kasten passt jeweils zu den Wortgruppen?

sound voice word sentence

a) loud, masculine, confident, singer's: ....
b) long, incomplete, complex, ungrammatical: ....
c) six-letter, French, expressive, technical: ....
d) familiar, musical, pleasant, knocking: ....

1.1.5.2 Sprechabsichten

1.1.5.2.1 *Auskunft*

1–2000

1. Übersetzen Sie.

a) Ich habe einen Ratschlag für dich.

....

b) Die Nachrichten sind sehr interessant.

....

c) Was bedeuten diese Informationen?

....

1–4000

2. Welches Verb aus dem Kasten passt? In manchen Fällen sind mehrere möglich.

explain	report	ask	make	recommend
show	give	answer	send	

a) .... a question
b) .... the news
c) .... some information
d) .... a remark
e) .... a few tips
f) .... some inquiries
g) .... a meaning
h) .... a statement
i) .... an answer
j) .... some interest
k) .... a message
l) .... a doctor
m) .... a report
n) .... some advice
o) .... an explanation

Zustimmung und Ablehnung 1.1.5.2.2

1–2000

1. Welche Antwort passt jeweils nicht? Kreuzen Sie das Kästchen an.

a) Are you coming with us?
- ☐ Yes, I am.
- ☐ No, not.
- ☐ No, I'm not.

b) Could I have the salt, please?
- ☐ Yes, of course.
- ☐ Certainly.
- ☐ Yes well.

c) You were wrong.
- ☐ I confess.
- ☐ Yes, it was my mistake.
- ☐ Yes, I admit it.

d) The answer is “Hadrian”.
- ☐ That’s incorrect.
- ☐ Wrong.
- ☐ Lie.

e) What do you think of nuclear energy?
- ☐ I mean it’s a good idea.
- ☐ I think it’s very clean.
- ☐ In my opinion, it’s dangerous.

f) I think this coffee’s a bit strong.
- ☐ Correct.
- ☐ Yes, it is.
- ☐ You’re right.

g) Are you for or against women’s rights?
- ☐ For.
- ☐ I’m in favour.
- ☐ In favour of.

2. Vervollständigen Sie die Antworten, um sie höflicher klingen zu lassen.

a)	– A cup of tea?	– Yes, ...
b)	– Sugar?	– No, ...
c)	– Are you staying with your sister?	– Yes, ...
d)	– Are you students?	– Yes, ...
e)	– Do you live here?	– Yes, ...
f)	– Is he English?	– No, ...
g)	– Do they like it?	– No, ...

2001–4000

3. Versuchen Sie, die unterstrichenen Wörter in dieser Klassendiskussion zu entwirren.

Teacher: Good morning, class. The subject of today’s discussion is nuclear energy. Timmy, what is your <u>iwev</u> on it? (. . . . .)

Timmy: I’m in <u>farvou</u> of it because it’s clean and efficient. (. . . . .)

Alison: I don’t <u>geare</u> at all. I think it’s dangerous – look at Chernobyl. (. . . . .)

Teacher: Would anyone like to <u>plyre</u> to that point? (. . . . .)

Frank: Yes, I’d like to <u>rectorc</u> it. If nuclear power is handled properly, it isn’t at all dangerous. (. . . . .)

Teacher:	So, Frank, you <u>proveap</u> of nuclear energy. (..........) Does anyone else <u>jobtec</u> to it? (..........)
Rachel:	Yes, I do. Although I <u>mirade</u> the technology, I don't think you can always rely on the people who work with it. (..........)
Peter:	I feel the same. In fact, I took part in a <u>rotpest</u> against the building of a new power station a few years ago. We were <u>prisaed</u> for our action in the local newspaper. (.........., ...)
Daniel:	Well, if you're going to <u>plocmain</u> about nuclear energy, where are we going to get our energy from in the future? (..........)
Francis:	We should cut down on the amount we use.
Teacher:	That's a good <u>grumenta</u>. Is that the answer to the problem, do you think, class? (..........)
Rachel:	I don't <u>dimn</u> cutting down on energy, but I think most people would <u>fusree</u> to cooperate. (.........., ...)
Teacher:	Well, perhaps we can continue this debate some other time. I don't think we're going to reach <u>meagrenet</u> today. Thank you, everybody. (..........)

Gewissheit und Zweifel 1.1.5.2.3

1–2000

1. Füllen Sie die Lücken mit den Wörtern aus dem Kasten. In manchen Fällen gibt es zwei mögliche Lösungen.

proof	sure	certainly	suppose
possible	probably	seem	
perhaps	impossible	probable	certain

Callum:	Has George been here?
Justin:	....
Callum:	What do you mean?
Justin:	Well, I'm not absolutely .... that he was here because I have no real .... of the fact, but since two cans of beer have disap-

peared from the fridge and nobody else has been here, it would ...., indeed ...., that he came home at some time this evening and has gone away again.
I .... haven't drunk the beer. But .... it was you?

Callum: .... – I've just come home from work.

Justin: So it must have been George.

Callum: I .... it was him. But how can we be ....?

2001–4000

2. In welche Spalte gehören die eingekreisten Wörter?

doubt
reality fact hesitate
possibility obvious decision
prove actually maybe guess
appear estimate clear

✓	?
certain	*uncertain*
....	....
....	....
....	....
....	....
....	....
....	....
....	....

3. Haken Sie jeweils das richtige Kästchen ab.

a) He is
☐ decided
☐ determined
☐ convinced to pass his driving test.

b) Have you
☐ decided
☐ estimated
☐ hesitated where you're going on holiday?

c) She ☐ doubts
☐ estimates
☐ claims to be related to the president.

Wertung und Urteil 1.1.5.2.4

1–2000

1. Geben Sie die Steigerungsformen folgender Adjektive an.

a) easy ....
b) nice ....
c) good ....
d) bad ....
e) difficult ....
f) great ....

1–4000

2. Ersetzen Sie das unterstrichene Wort durch sein Gegenteil.

a) It was a <u>good</u> (..........) performance.
b) His paintings are quite <u>extraordinary</u> (..........).
c) That was the most <u>interesting</u> (..........) film I've seen.
d) What was your <u>best</u> (..........) mark in your school report?
e) I preferred the <u>simple</u> (..........) questions.
f) That's a <u>useful</u> (..........) piece of information.
g) All the books you chose are <u>valuable</u> (..........).
h) He thinks it's an <u>important</u> (..........) work of art.
i) She didn't do too <u>well</u> (..........) in the golf tournament.

2001–4000

3. Unterstreichen Sie das passende Wort.

a) Don is very sensitive – he can't take any *critic/criticism.*
b) I'm so sorry – it was my *failure/fault.*
c) Why are you looking so *satisfactory/satisfied* with yourself?
d) He thinks his English is *ideal/perfect.*
e) We all hope your new job *proves/improves* interesting.
f) Would ten o'clock be *convenient/considerable* for you?
g) Would Friday be *practical/suitable* for me to come round?
h) The food was *excellent/extraordinary.* We all enjoyed it.

4. Welches Adjektiv aus dem Kasten passt jeweils?

precious	lovely	false	slight
boring	suitable	convenient	terrible

a) .... conversation, book, person
b) .... time, place, office hours
c) .... accident, sight, lie
d) .... face, present, voice
e) .... metal, object, ring
f) .... partner, home, school
g) .... statement, alarm, answer
h) .... accent, fever, pain

5. Setzen Sie das Verb in der richtigen Form ein (Infinitiv oder ing-Form) und fügen Sie – wo nötig – eine Präposition (for usw.) hinzu.

a) It's useless .... (say) anything – she won't listen.
b) I don't think it was proper of him .... (mention) how rich he was.
c) Would it suit you .... (come) at the weekend?
d) What was your purpose .... (*Präp.* + fly) there?
e) I'm just checking .... (see) if all the lights are off.
f) She proved .... (be) very helpful.
g) I was criticised .... (*Präp.* + come) late.
h) Do you think they made a good choice .... (*Präp.* + buy) a villa in France?
i) You deserve .... (get) a medal for all your work.

1.1.5.2.5 *Befehl und Verbot*

1–4000

1. Versuchen Sie, die Sätze jeweils unter Benutzung des eingeklammerten Wortes umzuformulieren.

a) He wouldn't let me go to the party.
I wasn't .... (allow).
b) I was forced to stay at home and clean up.
He .... (make).
c) Then I was told to go to bed.
Then he .... (order).

d) He forbade me to read in bed.
He .... (allow).
e) I always do what he tells me.
I always .... (obey).

2. Setzen Sie die richtige Verbform ein und fügen Sie – wo nötig – die entsprechende Präposition bzw. Partikel (*to, from* usw.) hinzu.

a) The teacher made me .... (write) six pages of English.
b) My father warned us .... (not, swim) in the pool.
c) They couldn't prevent the building .... (collapse).
d) We were given permission .... (paint) the house.
e) Mrs May let us .... (read) comics in class today.
f) I told you .... (not, talk) to him.
g) We have our hair .... (cut) at home.
h) She insisted .... (buy) me a drink.

Wunsch und Bitte 1.1.5.2.6

1–4000

1. Welcher Satz stimmt jeweils nicht? Kreuzen Sie das entsprechende Kästchen an.

a) ☐ I asked Jane help me.
☐ I asked Jane to help me.
☐ I asked Jane for her help.

b) ☐ I suggest we eat at home.
☐ I suggest eating at home.
☐ I suggest to eat at home.

c) ☐ I wish I would be on holiday.
☐ I wish I were on holiday.
☐ I wish I was on holiday.

d) ☐ She wants it done today.
☐ She wants it be done today.
☐ She wants it to be done today.

e) ☐ What was his last request before he died?
☐ What was his last wish before he died?
☐ What was his last demand before he died?

f) ☐ Our aim is to reach Phoenix tonight.
☐ Our will is to reach Phoenix tonight.
☐ Our wish is to reach Phoenix tonight.

1.1.5.2.7 *Begrüßung und Abschied*

1–4000

1. Wie lautet die richtige zeitliche Reihenfolge? Beginnen Sie am Vormittag.

Good evening!
Good afternoon!
Good morning!
Good night!

....

2. Wie würde man sie anreden?

a) Frau Humphrey (verheiratet): ....
b) Frau Stevens (ledig): ....
c) Frau Smith (Familienstand unbekannt): ....
d) Herr Bartlett (verheiratet): ....
e) Herr Johnson (ledig): ....

1.1.5.3 Häufige Redewendungen

1–2000

1. Welche Dialoghälften aus der linken und rechten Spalte passen jeweils zusammen?

a) I'm sorry.	p) Help yourself!
b) Thank you.	q) I said, where is it?
c) What's the matter?	r) All right.
d) Is he coming?	s) That's all right.
e) Sorry?	t) Never mind.
f) How are you?	u) Yes, please.
g) Would you like some?	v) Nothing.
h) Shall we go?	w) Fine, thanks.
i) Have a seat.	x) I hope so.
j) Could I please try some?	y) Thank you.
k) Oh, I've broken it.	z) Not at all.

2. Wie sagt man es auf Englisch?

a) Man fordert jemanden auf, sich zu bedienen:

....

b) Man möchte wissen, wieviel die Äpfel kosten.

....

c) Man fragt, ob jemand etwas Tee möchte.

....

d) Man bittet jemanden, aufzustehen.

....

e) Man bedankt sich.

....

f) Man entschuldigt sich.

....

g) Man hat etwas nicht gehört.

....

h) Man fragt, wie es jemandem geht.

....

i) Man fragt, was los ist.

....

2001–4000

3. Übersetzen Sie.

a) Viel Spaß!

....

b) – Ich bin müde. – Ich auch.

....

c) – Ich mag ihn. – Ich auch.

....

d) Oje!

....

e) Lass uns in Ruhe!

....

f) Raus!

....

g) Hau ab!

....

h) Bitte schön!

....

i) – Ich bin nicht müde. – Ich auch nicht.

....

j) – Ich mag es nicht. – Ich auch nicht.

....

1.1.6 *Der Mensch und die Gesellschaft*

1.1.6.1 Identifizierung

1–2000

1. Wie bezeichnet man sie?

a) .... e) ....
b) .... f) ....
c) .... g) ....
d) .... h) ....

1–4000

2. Wie lautet die Pluralform?

a) gentleman .... d) baby ....
b) lady .... e) woman ....
c) child .... f) person ....

2001–4000

3. Vervollständigen Sie diesen Dialog.

Girl: .... your name?
Boy: Jeremy.
Girl: Jeremy – that's a nice .... And what's your ....?
Boy: Postlethwaite.
Girl: Hm. What do you .... your dog?
Boy: Mortimer.
Girl: So it's .... Mortimer Postlethwaite?
Boy: I suppose so.
Girl: That's a big .... for such a little dog. What .... is it – is it a he or a she?
Boy: Well, with a name like Mortimer, he's got to be ...., hasn't he?

Familie 1.1.6.2

1–4000

Meet the family

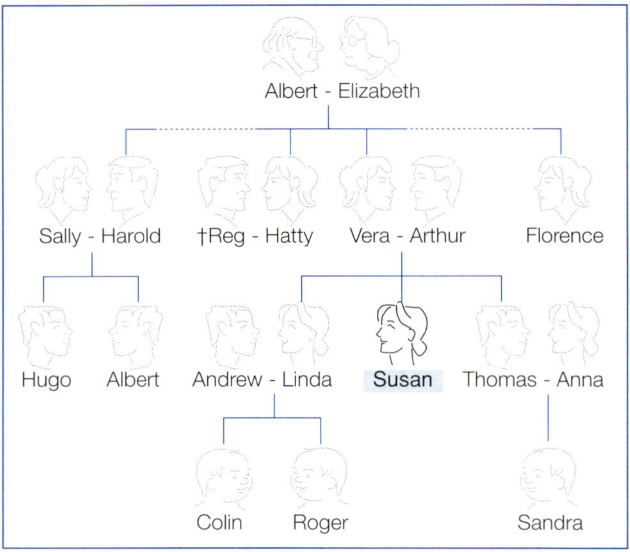

1. Wie werden die Familienmitglieder genannt?

a) Elizabeth and Albert are Susan's . . . .
b) Susan's . . . . is called Thomas.
c) Anna is her . . . .
d) Sandra is the . . . . of Thomas and Anna.
e) Andrew and Linda have two . . . .
f) Colin and Roger are Sandra's . . . .
g) Reg and Harold are Susan's . . . .
h) Florence is Vera's . . . . and Susan's . . . .
i) Susan's . . . . and . . . . are called Vera and Arthur.
j) Hugo's . . . . Albert has the same name as his . . . .
k) Linda's . . . . is Andrew.
l) Andrew's . . . . are Vera and Arthur.
m) Susan's . . . . Reg died five years ago, so Hatty is a . . . .
n) Susan has two . . . . (Colin and Roger) and one . . . . (Sandra).
o) Albert and Elizabeth have four children and five . . . .
p) Linda and Susan are their . . . . and Hugo, Albert and Thomas are their . . . .
q) Sally is Harold's . . . .
r) Sally and Harold are the . . . . of Hugo and Albert.

2. Füllen Sie die Lücken mit Hilfe der Wörter aus dem Kasten.

couple engaged married single
bride (2x) groom relative heir

The Wedding Day

It was a lovely wedding with about 100 guests – most of them . . . . .s of the happy . . . . who both have large families. The . . . . wore a long white dress and the . . . . was in a blue suit. A lot of the guests were young, ... people, but there were also . . . . couples with children. After the speeches, the . . . .'s father announced that his other daughter had just got . . . . to the groom's brother. The new father-in-law must have felt very happy for his daughters, because both young men are . . . . .s to a large fortune.

Soziale Bindungen 1.1.6.3

1–4000

1. Fügen Sie das Wort mit der gegenteiligen Bedeutung in die jeweilige Lücke ein.

a) Rosa has a <u>boyfriend</u> but Gerry hasn't got a . . . .
b) He's always had lots of <u>friends</u>, never any . . . .
c) They used to be business <u>rivals</u>, but now they're . . . .
d) I tried to keep the affair <u>private</u>, but she's made it very . . . . by talking to the newspapers.
e) The countries have a . . . . language but very <u>different</u> accents.

2. Unterstreichen Sie das passende Wort.

a) The gardens have been opened to the *public/society.*
b) Aunt Geraldine enjoys the *company/society* of young men.
c) France is quite a mixed *people/society.*
d) The *people/society* living on the islands speak the same dialect.
e) Have you met Gilbert? He's a *colleague/companion* from work.
f) Is she a *fellow/member* of the club?
g) I've told the children not to talk to *enemies/strangers.*
h) My mother does a lot of work for the *community/society.*

1.1.6.4 Berufe

1–4000

1. Was sind sie?

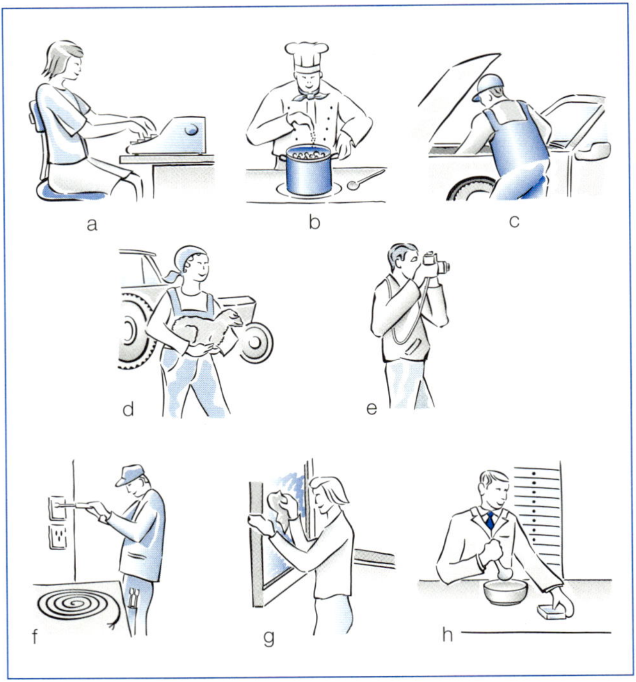

a) She's a	e) He's a ....
b) He's a	f) He's an ....
c) He's a	g) She's a ....
d) She's a	h) He's a ....

2. Übersetzen Sie.

a) Meine Schwester ist Sekretärin.

....

b) Mein Schwager ist Geschäftsmann.

....

c) Ich möchte Ingenieurin werden.

....

d) Meine Onkel sind alle Metzger oder Schneider.

....

e) Ich bin Praktikant.

....

2001–4000

3. Fügen Sie die fehlenden Wörter ein.
Der erste Buchstabe ist als Hilfe angegeben.

a) A lady in a top commercial job is a b...........
b) Somebody who tries to sell things is a s...........
c) Somebody who plays a sport for money is a p...........
d) Somebody who is learning a job is a t........... or an a...........

Soziale Situation 1.1.6.5

1–4000

1. Welche Beschreibung in der rechten Spalte passt jeweils zu den Wörtern in der linken?

a) poor	s) he is in charge of meetings; he is usually sitting down
b) service	t) a status in society and in the military
c) wealthy	u) something useful offered to people, organisations etc.
d) beggar	v) somebody who belongs to a town or a country
e) chairman	w) somebody in charge of a business, a department, an organisation etc.
f) boss	x) somebody asking for money in the street
g) rank	y) it describes someone who has a lot of money
h) citizen	z) a word to describe people who have very little money

a) .... c) .... e) .... g) ....
b) .... d) .... f) .... h) ....

1.1.6.6 Soziales Verhalten

1–2000

1. Trennen Sie die Buchstaben an den richtigen Stellen, so dass ein sinnvoller Satz entsteht.

a) Itisacustomheretogiveguests thebiggestbed.

....

b) Howmanyfamiliesliveinthisneighbourhood?

....

c) Whenareyougoingtovisityourgrandparents?

....

d) Ihaveapresentforyou.

....

e) Congratulationsonpassingyourtest!

....

f) Hesayshehasinvitedfiftypeopletohisparty.

....

g) Doyouhavemanysocialproblemsinthisarea?

....

2. Versuchen Sie, die Wörter in die richtige Reihenfolge zu bringen, um sinnvolle Sätze zu bilden.

a) me show let where you room is your

....

b) coming party the you are to ?

....

c) again time can meet we some ?

....

d) colleague I've evening from work got this date a with a

....

e) think see go and I doctor a should you

....

2001–4000

3. Unterstreichen Sie das passende Wort.

a) Let's have a drink to *celebrate/congratulate* the birth of your son!
b) The children *bowed/waved* out of the window as the car left.
c) I've got an *appointment/invitation* to a garden party at Buckingham Palace.

d) We have two new girls *joining/taking part in* the class this year.
e) Let me *greet/introduce* you to our friends.
f) They're *getting along/getting divorced* with each other.
g) When is the *marriage/wedding* going to be?
h) Will you show our *hosts/visitors* their bedroom?
i) Have you had any *contact/kiss* with her?

4. In diesen Sätzen steckt jeweils ein Fehler. Versuchen Sie, ihn auszubessern.

a) I'm getting married with my boyfriend next summer.
b) Welcome in London!
c) May I introduce you my father?
d) He is a very good hostess.
e) Only twenty people took part at the competition.
f) The crowds waved us to.
g) After ten years of marriage, they are now separate.

Schicksal und Zufall 1.1.7

1–2000

1. Füllen Sie die Lücken mit Hilfe der Wörter aus dem Kasten. Setzen Sie – wo nötig – die Verben in die entsprechende Zeitform.

save happen lucky (2x) dangerous
fire trouble safety
lose luck famous succeed

Clive: Tell me what ....
Mary: There was a .... in the forest and we didn't know what to do.
Clive: That must have been very ....
Mary: Yes, we got into real .... because we .... our way.
Clive: How awful!
Mary: Yes, but we were very .... A local forester heard us shouting for help. He .... in finding us and took us to ....
Clive: That was amazing ....

Mary: Yes, he .... our lives. It was in all the newspapers.
Clive: So you're ....!
Mary: And very .... to be alive!

1–4000

2. Wie lautet das Gegenteil?

a) luck ....
b) success ....
c) danger ....
d) safe ....
e) destroy ....
f) creation ....
g) fortunately ....
h) lose ....

2001–4000

3. Versuchen Sie, die Wortfragmente in den zwei Spalten sinnvoll zu verbinden, z. B. ergibt oc- und *-casion* das Wort *occasion*.

a) mys-	....	-gency
b) oppor-	....	-ation
c) emer-	....	-plode
d) diffi-	....	-casion
e) situ-	....	-ately
f) res-	....	-tage
g) ex-	....	-ture
h) de-	....	-dition
i) oc-	....	-cue
j) adven-	....	-tunity
k) fortun-	....	-tery
l) con-	....	-culty
m) advan-	....	-stroy

4. Welches Wort passt jeweils nicht?

a) chance, risk, mystery, opportunity ....
b) damage, advantage, harm, destruction ....
c) condition, emergency, state, situation ....
d) difficulty, blow, event, bad luck ....

5. Fügen Sie die richtige Präposition ein.

a) There's no chance .... him winning the race now.
b) I met them .... chance.
c) I think you did it .... purpose.
d) Ring him up .... case he doesn't know.

e) .... lack of money he began begging in the streets.
f) The end of the marriage was a terrible blow .... him.
g) It was an occasion .... remembering friends who live far away.
h) It's a rare opportunity .... drive such an old car.

Alltagswelt 1.2

Der Mensch und sein Zuhause 1.2.1

Haus und Wohnung 1.2.1.1

1–2000

1. Wie heißt es?

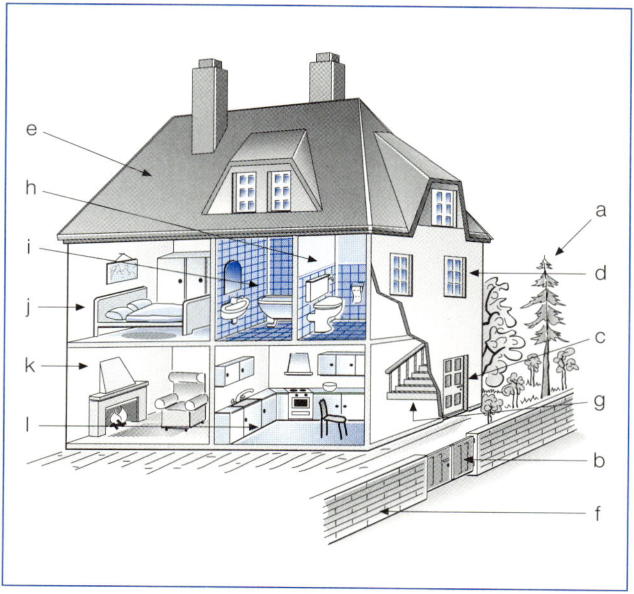

a) ....
b) ....
c) ....
d) ....
e) ....
f) ....
g) ....
h) ....
i) ....
j) ....
k) ....
l) ....

2. Wie würde man es auf Amerikanisch sagen?

a) ground floor ....
first floor ....
second floor ....

b) They've moved into a new flat.
....

c) Let's take the lift.
....

d) Where's the toilet?
....

2001–4000

3. Füllen Sie die Lücken mit Hilfe der Wörter aus dem Kasten.

paint	front	storeys	chimneys
cracks	furnished	ceiling	basement
upstairs	dining room	move	

Moving

The house is lovely. It's on three ...., with the kitchen down in the .... and a large .... next to it. The living room on the ground floor has a lovely stucco .... and is beautifully .... there are three bedrooms. The .... of the house is in Cotswold stone and has a heavy oak door. On the roof are two large, attractive ...., but they've got a few .... so they would have to be repaired. Also, the front door needs a little .... But apart from that, it's a beautiful, comfortable house. It's a pity we've got to .... out into a caravan at the end of the month.

Einrichtung 1.2.1.2

1–2000

1. Wovon ist hier die Rede?

a) It usually has four legs and a back: ....
b) You lie in it: ....
c) You keep food and other things in it: ....
d) You eat at it: ....
e) You write at it: ....
f) You find it in a park: ....
g) A word for tables, chairs, beds etc.: ....

2001–4000

2. Welches Wort passt jeweils nicht?

a) cooker, wardrobe, fridge, oven: ....
b) armchair, curtain, sofa, couch: ....
c) blanket, lamp, pillow, cushion: ....
d) wardrobe, chest of drawers, stove, shelves: ....

3. Vervollständigen Sie die Sätze mit Hilfe der Wörter aus dem Kasten.

blanket	cushion	pillow	oven
fridge	armchair	sofa	
wardrobe	carpet	freezer	drawer

a) You keep food cool in a ....
b) You freeze food in a ....
c) You bake bread and cakes in an ....
d) You hang clothes in a ....
e) Your lay your head on a .... in bed.
f) Some people like to keep warm under a .... in bed.
g) An .... is a comfortable piece of furniture.
h) A .... is for more than one person to sit on.
i) Many people like a .... on the living room floor.
j) You can keep small objects in a ....
k) Soft ....s are usually found on sofas or in armchairs.

1.2.1.3 Gegenstände und Geräte

1–4000

1. Fügen Sie die richtigen Wortfragmente zusammen.

cil bag point brella
et ket chief dle
let driver der sors

a) lad. . . . .
b) hand. . . . .
c) scis. . . . .
d) um. . . . .
e) can. . . . .
f) bas. . . . .
g) pen. . . . .
h) screw. . . . .
i) buck. . . . .
j) wal. . . . .
k) ball. . . . .
l) handker. . . . .

2. **Mrs Clumsy ist im Großmarkt mit ihrem Einkaufswagen gegen ein wackeliges Regal gestoßen und es sind allerhand Haushaltswaren heruntergestürzt. Gleichzeitig hat sie ihre Handtasche fallen lassen, deren Inhalt nun ebenfalls auf dem Boden verstreut liegt. Welche Gegenstände gehören höchstwahrscheinlich nicht in die Handtasche? Übersetzen Sie diese dann ins Deutsche.**

handkerchief pen light bulb scales needle
ladder
clock purse saw wastepaper basket
hose box of screws
rope mirror key glasses

englisch	*deutsch*
. . . .	. . . .
. . . .	. . . .
. . . .	. . . .
. . . .	. . . .
. . . .	. . . .
. . . .	. . . .
. . . .	. . . .
. . . .	. . . .
. . . .	. . . .

3. Übersetzen Sie.

a) Wo ist meine Brille?

....

b) Ich brauche einen Spiegel und eine Schere.

....

c) Diese Waage ist digital.

....

4. Wie lautet die richtige Reihenfolge? Fangen Sie jeweils mit dem kleinsten Gegenstand an.

a) rope, thread, string

....

b) scissors, saw, needle

....

c) wallet, basket, handbag

....

d) nail, key, needle

....

e) ashtray, match, lighter

....

Sauberkeit 1.2.1.4

1–4000

1. Welche Wörter aus dem Kasten fehlen? Setzen Sie die Verben – wo nötig – in die richtige Zeitform.

broom	dust	dishwasher	sweep
wash	polish	clean	
tidy	dirty	mess	washing machine
laundry	stain	wipe	

This house is so ...., and the living room is a .... too! I want you to have it all .... and .... by tonight. You can start by putting all those cups and dishes in the .... Then you can do the .... – fill the .... up with all your shirts and then do a white wash. And just look at those ....s on the table-cloth – you'd better wash that as well. And after you've

.... the furniture you can .... the dining-room table until I can see my face in it. When you've done the dusting, ... all the kitchen surfaces with a damp cloth. Finally, there's a new .... in the cupboard – you can use it to .... the steps. And don't forget to .... your hands before you start preparing tonight's meal.

1.2.2 *Kleidung und Schmuck*

1–2000

1. Wovon ist hier die Rede?

pocket skirt shirt shoes

trousers dress coat

jacket hat watch suit

glove ring buttons

1. Um welche Wörter aus dem Kasten geht es hier?

a) You wear it on your finger: ....
b) You wear it on your hand: ....
c) They have two legs: ....
d) You wear it on your head: ....
e) You wear them on your feet: ....
f) You wear it on your wrist: ....
g) You wear it over a shirt: ....
h) A jacket and trousers together: ....
i) It hangs from the waist: ....
j) You wear it over your other clothes: ....
k) You wear it under a jacket: ....
l) You can keep a handkerchief in it: ....
m) You close a jacket, coat etc. with them: ....
n) Brides often wear a white one: ....

2001–4000

2. Wie heißt es?

a)	g) ....
b)	h) ....
c)	i) ....
d)	j) ....
e)	k) ....
f)	l) ....

1–4000

3. Vervollständigen Sie die Sätze mit den Verben aus dem Kasten. Setzen Sie sie – wo nötig – in die richtige Zeitform.

wear change put on sew
try on fit knit take off

a) I don't think these trousers .... They're too tight.
b) Do you want to .... a larger size?
c) I've .... an extra pair of socks because these shoes are too big.
d) My Hubert .... on all his buttons himself and mends holes in his socks. He even .... me a lovely woollen scarf and a pair of gloves for the winter.
e) .... your sweater so that I can see the blouse properly.
f) He goes to the office by bicycle, so he has to shower and .... before he starts work.
g) What shall I .... today?

1.2.3 *Arbeitswelt*

1.2.3.1 Fabrik und Werkstatt

1–4000

1. Versuchen Sie, die Wörter in die richtige Reihenfolge zu bringen, um sinnvolle Sätze zu bilden.

a) my repair you could today car ?
....
b) get to we'll parts spare have some
....
c) friendly and service the quick is very
....
d) tools with of has he workshop a lots
....
e) nations the richest industrial are the
....
f) ten fix to took it minutes him window the
....

g) brother the furniture road down works factory in the my

. . . .

h) they are mend to toilet the when going ?

. . . .

Wirtschaftsleben 1.2.3.2

Allgemeines 1.2.3.2.1

1–2000

1. Wie könnte man es mit Hilfe der Wörter im Kasten anders ausdrücken? Setzen Sie – wo nötig – die Verben in die richtige Zeitform.

pay wages sale busy
business unemployed goods
firm offer order

a) He hasn't got a job. He's . . . .
b) I've got too much work to do. I'm too . . . .
c) They don't pay me very much. My . . . . are quite low.
d) They've reduced all the prices. They're having a . . . .
e) I'd like you to send me a hundred packets. Could I . . . . a hundred packets?
f) She said I could have the job. She has . . . . me the job.
g) How much money do you get? What's the . . . . like?
h) He wants to work for another company. He wants to change . . . . s.
i) I want to be my own boss. I'm going to start my own . . . .
j) We import a lot of things. We use a lot of imported . . . .

2001–4000

2. Welche Substantive sind mit den Verben verwandt?

a) produce ....
b) manage ....
c) compete ....
d) employ ....

3. Unterstreichen Sie das passende Wort.

a) It's a report on the *economic/economical* situation in Egypt.
b) I got it for £25. It was a real *bargain/deal.*
c) We have to pay tax on the *imports/exports* we receive.
d) *Trade/Economy* between the two continents has grown.
e) The factory is her *possession/property.*
f) *Demand/Supply* for mobile phones is rising fast.
g) After 40 years in *employment/labour,* he is going to retire this December.
h) Only 500 of these record players were *produced/provided* in the factory.
i) Could I speak to the *head/manager,* please?

1.2.3.2.2 *Geschäft*

1–4000

1. Versuchen Sie, diese Nonsensworte zu entwirren und die richtigen Wortteile zusammenzusetzen. Fügen Sie dann die deutsche Übersetzung hinzu.

superping shopment drugtising
adverstore departmarket

a) super.......... ....
b) shop.......... ....
c) drug.......... ....
d) adver.......... ....
e) depart.......... ....

2. Fügen Sie die Verben in der richtigen Zeitform ein.

a) I .... (buy) these clothes from a department store yesterday.
b) We .... (sell) our car two days after it was advertised.
c) My grandfather .... (deal in) military medals for over forty years before he died.

Geld *1.2.4*

1–2000

1. Welches der eingeklammerten Worte passt jeweils? Unterstreichen Sie es.

a) I'd like to pay by .... *(money/bill/cash)*
b) What's the .... of petrol these days? *(rent/price/tax)*
c) She .... hundreds of pounds on clothes every month. *(pays/costs/spends)*
d) I'm .... all my money for a new bike. *(earning/saving/spending)*
e) He .... it all on his girlfriend. *(saved/spent/paid)*

2. Welche Präposition fehlt?

a) There are 100 pence .... a pound.
b) The rent .... their flat is very low.
c) The cost .... running a car is too high for me.
d) My father has no money. He's been .... debt all his adult life.
e) Can you give me four five-pound notes .... a twenty?
f) How much money have you got .... the bank?

3. Ersetzen Sie das unterstrichene Wort durch sein Gegenteil aus dem Kasten.

buy	cash	spend	save	expensive

a) We went to a very <u>cheap</u> restaurant and had an excellent meal. ....
b) You <u>earn</u> far more than me. ....
c) We want to <u>rent</u> a three-bedroomed flat. ....

d) He's finds it hard to <u>spend</u> money. . . . .
e) They don't take <u>cheques</u>. . . . .

2001–4000

4. Vervollständigen Sie die Sätze mit den Wörtern aus dem Kasten.

interest	loan	owe	afford
hire	coins	charge	value
insurance	income	profit	currency

a) Have you got any change? I need some . . . . for the ticket machine.
b) I want to borrow some money from the bank. I'll have to ask the bank manager for a . . . .
c) If I leave this money in the account for a year, how much will I earn? What is the . . . . rate?
d) I lent you some money last month. You . . . . me $30.
e) Where can I get some foreign . . . . ? I've got to change pounds into pesetas and lire.
f) He says he can't . . . . to eat in restaurants – he hasn't got the money.
g) There's an extra . . . . for breakfast. It will cost you £11.
h) They made a lot of money from selling the house. In fact, they made a . . . . of £50,000.
i) They both work and they don't have any children. They're DINKs – "dual . . . . , no kids".
j) You don't have to buy skis – you can . . . . them from one of the shops.
k) You should take out . . . . on both cars, so that if anything happens you won't have to pay.
l) The sculpture cost me £4,000. I don't know what its . . . . is today.

5. Wie lautet die Präposition?

to	on (3x)	in	of	per (2x)

a) How much money have you got .... your account?
b) If you take out a loan, you have to pay interest .... the amount that you borrow.
c) Are you paid .... day or .... hour?
d) Washing machines have been reduced .... 60 per cent of their original price.
e) I have to pay 7 per cent .... my income into National Insurance.
f) I've never bought anything .... credit. I don't like to owe money.
g) The company made a big loss .... a business deal with Malaysia.

Ämter und Behörden 1.2.5

1–4000

1. Welche Dialoghälften aus der linken und rechten Spalte passen jeweils zusammen?

a) I'm looking for Mr Bertram's office.	u) No, I think they should have appointed Roger.
b) I think I've filled in everything on the form.	v) Was there a long queue?
c) About 300 staff are going to lose their jobs.	w) I'm sure they won't even look at your application.
d) I went to register Kay with the kindergarten.	x) He's moved to another department.
e) Do you think that was a responsible decision?	y) Is that official?
f) I'm applying for the office of mayor.	z) Have you signed it?

a) .... c) .... e) ....
b) .... d) .... f) ....

1.2.6 *Post- und Fernmeldewesen*

1.2.6.1 Post

1–2000

1. Wie heißt es?

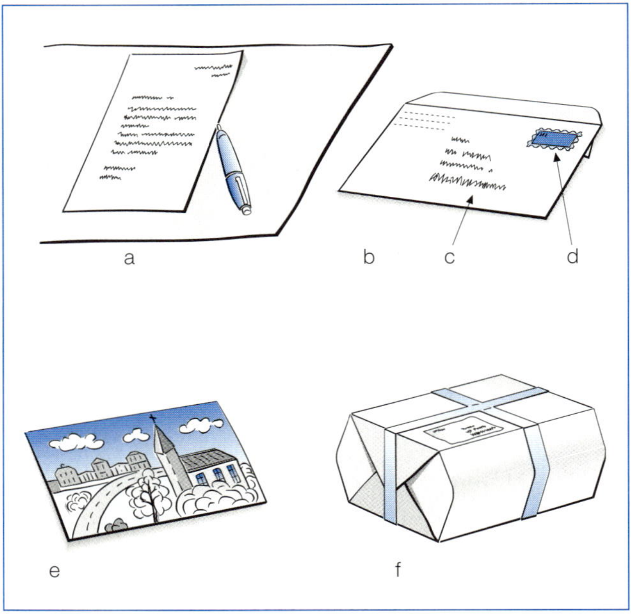

a) . . . .
b) . . . .
c) . . . .
d) . . . .
f) . . . .
f) . . . .

1–4000

2. Sie wollen einen Brief nach Kanada schicken. Was machen Sie?

letterbox post post office
letter envelope airmail
stamp address (2x) sender postage

First of all, I write the .... Then I put it in an ...., write the .... in Canada on it and the ....'s .... on the back. Then I put a .... and an .... sticker on it and take it to the nearest .... to .... it. If I don't know what the .... for Canada is, I go to the .... and find out. Then I wait for a reply!

Telefon

1.2.6.2

1–4000

1. Fügen Sie die richtigen Wortteile aus der linken und rechten Spalte zusammen und übersetzen Sie dann die Ausdrücke.

	deutsch	
a) hang	....	box
b) phone..........	....	call
c) tele..........	....	phone
d) local	....	card
e) phone	....	up

2. Welche Wörter fehlen?

a) If you want to make a phone call, you need some coins or a ....
b) If you have problems making the call, you can ring the ....
c) Local calls are cheaper after 6 o'clock and .... calls are cheaper after 8.
d) I've been trying to ring her for an hour, but she's still ....
e) You can call me or send a .... – the number's the same.
f) He's locked himself into his flat and won't .... the phone.
g) You don't have to .... the number again – you just press the redial button.

1.2.7 *Rechtswesen*

1.2.7.1 Rechtsprechung

1–4000

1. Unterstreichen Sie jeweils das richtige Wort.

a) The police *searched/arrested/claimed* a woman in her twenties.
b) She was taken to *justice/trial/court*.
c) She finally *confessed/swore/denied* to having stolen the car.
d) The *justice/judge/lawyer* sentenced her to six months in jail.
e) She promised never to break the *legal/justice/law* again.

2. Durch welchen Ausdruck aus dem Kasten könnte man den unterstrichenen jeweils ersetzen?

jail — prisoners — punishment — accused of — verdict

a) The sentence was five years of hard labour.
b) The youth was charged with insulting a policeman.
c) The convicts are allowed to exercise in the yard for an hour a day.
d) Has life in prison improved?
e) A judgment was passed on the third day of the trial.

3. Wie heißt es richtig?

a) The police *is/are* at the door.
b) In this country, the police *doesn't/don't* earn much.
c) If you see the police, make sure *he doesn't/they don't* see you.
d) Ask the policeman if *he knows/they know* the way.

Strafbares Verhalten

1–4000

1. Welches Verb aus dem Kasten passt jeweils?

swindle	rob	kill
shoot	steal	force

a) .... a bank, a train, somebody
b) .... someone dead, through a window, at someone
c) .... a car, a watch, money, to pay for drugs
d) .... the taxman, somebody out of something
e) .... somebody, an animal, a victim
f) .... somebody to give you money, somebody into the back of a car, somebody to lie down

2. Setzen Sie die Wörter aus dem Kasten in die richtige Spalte.

steal	robber	kill	thief
murder	robbery	violence	offence
shoot	burglar	criminal	murder

person	*crime*	*verb*
....	....	....
....	....	....
....	....	....
....	....	....

3. Vervollständigen Sie die Sätze mit den Wörtern aus dem Kasten. Setzen Sie das Verb – wo nötig – in die richtige Form.

violent	wrong	robbery	guilty
murder	illegal	suspect	
steal	shot	force	

a) I heard somebody shooting. There were several ....s.
b) That's the thief. He .... the painting.
c) You shouldn't have done that. It was ....
d) You're not allowed to sell alcohol to anyone under 18. It's ....
e) He killed two policemen. He committed a double ....
f) He threatened violence, and he became very ....
g) She used force to open the door. She .... the door open.
h) He was one of the robbers. He took part in the ....
i) They suspect her of stealing the car. She is the main ....
j) They proved that he had committed the crime. He was found ....

1.2.8 *Arzt und Krankenhaus*

1–4000

1. Bringen Sie die Ereignisse in die richtige Reihenfolge, indem Sie die Kästchen nummerieren.

- ☐ She said Monty needed medical treatment fast.
- ☐ So the tour leader called for an ambulance.
- ☐ The doctors gave him a drug to fight the poison.
- ☐ Monty was bitten by a poisonous snake while on holiday.
- ☐ He was quickly cured and able to join the group again.
- ☐ It arrived very quickly and Monty was rushed to hospital.
- ☐ Fortunately, one of the women in the group was a nurse.
- ☐ But he had to take pills for the rest of the holiday.

2. Versuchen Sie, die unterstrichenen Ausdrücke zu entwirren.

a) He hates going to the <u>titdens</u>, but he won't stop eating sweets. ....
b) I'm afraid you will have to have an <u>perotiona</u> on both eyes. ....
c) I went to my doctor, and he sent me straight to a <u>cepsiastil</u>. ....
d) She's wealthy. She can afford the best <u>genosur</u> in the country. ....

e) We sat in the <u>ingtawi omor</u> for two hours. ....
....
f) Don't forget to take your <u>dicemeni</u> before dinner.
....
g) There are too many doctors for the number of <u>tienpats</u> in this part of the country. ....
h) I don't take any medicine – I think it's all <u>snipoo</u>.
....

Schule und Universität 1.2.9

1–2000

1. Welches Verb aus dem Kasten passt jeweils?

translate	learn	teach	study

a) .... a class, a lesson, a course, at a school
b) .... French, a subject, at university, hard
c) .... a language, to speak English, by listening
d) .... a letter, a book, from German into English

2. Was sind sie?

a) She's a .... She studies chemistry and biology at Hamburg University.
b) They're third-year .... They go to the Manor School.
c) He wants to be a .... He wants to teach children in West Africa.

2001–4000

3. Um welche Fächer geht es hier?

a) It is the study of numbers: ....
b) It is the study of our physical universe: ....
c) It is the study of our natural surroundings: ....
d) It is the study of the past: ....
e) It is the study of chemical substances: ....
f) It is the study of plants and animals: ....

1–4000

4. In diesem Buchstabenquadrat sind zehn Wörter aus dem Bereich der Bildung versteckt. Versuchen Sie sie aufzufinden, indem Sie von oben nach unten und von links nach rechts lesen.

g	f	s	d	s	c	h	o	o	l
x	g	t	i	d	e	l	s	g	o
e	d	u	c	a	t	i	o	n	d
x	i	d	t	d	n	r	o	t	b
a	c	y	i	o	r	p	w	e	r
m	k	h	o	m	e	w	o	r	k
i	r	a	n	o	p	s	r	m	t
t	t	s	a	t	o	p	i	c	l
b	a	t	r	e	r	k	a	o	q
u	w	e	y	l	t	e	a	c	h

5. *Take, pass* oder *fail*? Welches Verb passt? Setzen Sie es – wo nötig – in die richtige Zeitform ein.

a) "You have .... your geography exam for the third time. What is your excuse?" asked the headmistress.
b) If you don't .... this time, you'll be thrown out of university.
c) – Have you got a driving licence?
– No, I've never .... a driving test.
d) Hooray! I've .... my English test!

Interessen 1.3

Kunst 1.3.1

Bildende Kunst 1.3.1.1

1–4000

1. Versuchen Sie, die unterstrichenen Wörter in diesen Sätzen zu entwirren.

a) She can't tanip at all, but she's a very good torsculp.
. . . . , ...
b) I'm going to the sumume. There's an bixhitonei of ancient Greek jewellery. . . . . , ...
c) I don't like the lyste of this painting. Who is the trista?
. . . . , ...
d) We must hang some sticurep up on the walls. Is there a lagrely in town which isn't too expensive? . . . . ,
. . . .
e) It looks like a wardnig, but it's actually a trinp. . . . . ,
. . . .
f) He doesn't like tinpinagsn In fact, he doesn't like tar of any kind. . . . . , ...
g) Michelangelo was a great napiret, but he is probably more famous for his plustucers. . . . . , ...

2. Unterstreichen Sie jeweils das richtige Wort.

a) I *drawn/drew/painted* it with a pencil.
b) He's a very talented *sculpture/sculpter/sculptor*.
c) Van Gogh was a famous *drawer/printer/artist*.
d) We've just bought some Beryl Cook *draws/paints/prints*.

Theater, Film und Fernsehen 1.3.1.2

1–4000

1. Worum geht es hier?
Fügen Sie die Wörter aus dem Kasten ein.

audience	ticket	screen	stage
actor	cinema	plays	
scenes	comedy	acts	

a) Laurence Olivier was a famous one: ....
b) Shakespeare wrote lots of them: ....
c) You need one to get into a theatre or cinema: ....
d) Plays are usually performed on one: ....
e) The people watching a film or play etc.: ....
f) A film is made up of different ....
g) Classical plays usually have five: ....
h) Another word for a funny play: ....
i) A building where films are shown: ....
j) Films are shown on this: ....

2. Unterstreichen Sie das richtige Wort.

a) He has always wanted to *perform/play* on stage.
b) The *acts/scenes* in this movie change very fast.
c) There are five *performances/stages* of the play.
d) What was her *play/role* in the film?
e) How often do you go to the *movie/movies*?
f) It was supposed to be a *comedy/tragedy,* but there weren't many laughs from the audience.
g) It's a five-act *piece/play* by Tom Stoppard.
h) How many films has Woody Allen *directed/played*?

1.3.1.3 Musik

1–4000

1. Setzen Sie die Wörter aus dem Kasten in die richtige Spalte.

violin orchestra conductor
composer choir guitar
musician piano band

instruments	*professions*	*groups of musicians*
....	....	....
....	....	....
....	....	....

2. Vervollständigen Sie die Wörter.

a) There are some people who never listen to _ u _ i c.
b) I heard the _ u n _ on the radio this morning and I can't get it out of my head.
c) He loves music with a strong r _ y t _ m.
d) We're going to a _ o n _ e r _ at the Albert Hall tonight.
e) How many _ t _ i n _ s has a bass guitar got?
f) Do you play an i _ s _ _ u m _ _ t?
g) She's deaf, but she's very _ u s _ _ a l.
h) I can _ i _ g and I can _ l a _ the piano, but I can't do both at the same time.
i) Mary's a pop _ _ n g e _ and writes her own _ o n _ s.

Kommunikationsmittel 1.3.2

1–4000

1. Hier ist leider die Kommunikation etwas zusammengebrochen. Versuchen Sie, die Substantive zu entwirren und die richtigen Wortteile zusammenzusetzen.

broadview	pubcast	internel
chanzine	prolish	headvision
teleline	newsgramme	magapaper

a) broad..........
b) pub..........
c) inter..........
d) chan..........
e) pro..........
f) head..........
g) tele..........
h) news..........
i) maga..........

2. Welches Wort aus dem Kasten passt jeweils zu den Wortgruppen?

radio	press	media

a) ....: magazine, paper, print
b) ....: broadcast, channel, programme
c) ....: television, radio, press

3. Welches Wort passt? Unterstreichen Sie es.

a) Have you seen the latest *issue/magazine* of "Vogue"?
b) Which *broadcast/channel* is the football match on?
c) It was a *life/live* television interview.
d) He spends all his time writing. He has *printed/published* four novels already.
e) They *announced/published* his death on the nine o'clock news.

1.3.3 *Erholung und Freizeit*

1–4000

1.3.3.1 Erholung

1. Unterstreichen Sie das richtige Wort.

a) How often do you go *for/on* holiday?
b) I like to go *for/on* walks in the woods.
c) I like to *make/take* a break from work every two hours.
d) Why don't you *have/make* a rest?
e) We don't get much time *for/of* leisure.

1.3.3.2 Freizeitbeschäftigungen und Hobbys

1. Was machen sie? Vervollständigen Sie die Sätze.

a) He's taking a . . . .

b) They're . . . .

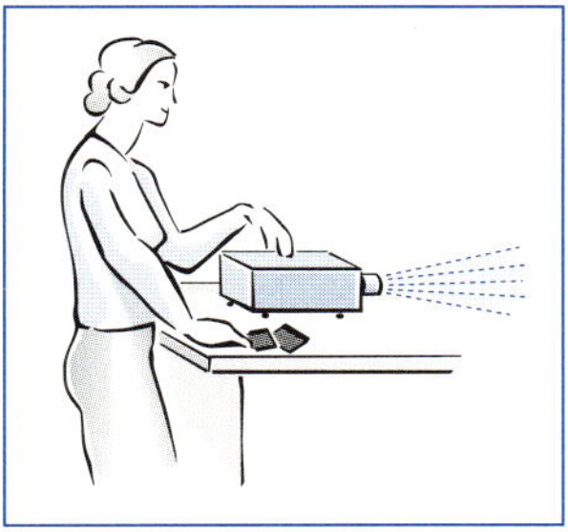

c) She's giving a . . . .
show.

d) They're . . . .
a mountain.

e) They're . . . .
in the garden.

f) He's . . . .

2. In jedem dieser Sätze steckt ein Fehler. Versuchen Sie, ihn zu verbessern.

a) Michael won a price for his essay on African elephants.
b) That's a lovely photography of your grandparents.
c) I think the last piece of this puzzle is missing.
d) I see you've got a new stereo set. Those boxes are very big!
e) They've gone wandering in the mountains.

3. Fügen Sie die Wörter aus dem Kasten in die richtige Spalte.

stereo slide tape print
camera speaker photograph
cassette recorder TV colour film

photography	*home entertainment*
....	....
....	....
....	....
....	....
....	....

1.3.3.3 Vergnügen und Genuss

1–4000

1. Welches Wort fehlt jeweils in diesen Sätzen?

a) She can't tell a .... without laughing.
b) He was very .... with his present and thanked everyone for it.
c) – We're going to the cinema.
   – Well, ... yourselves.
d) – Do you roll your own ....s?
   – Yes, I always buy .... in Holland and make my own.
e) – Do you smoke?
   – Not cigarettes, but ....s and a ....
f) In some countries there are now more women ....s than men.
g) – Did you .... the film?
   – Yes, it was very ....
h) The word infotainment is a fusion of information and ....

Sport

1.3.4

1–4000

1. Was machen sie? Vervollständigen Sie die Sätze.

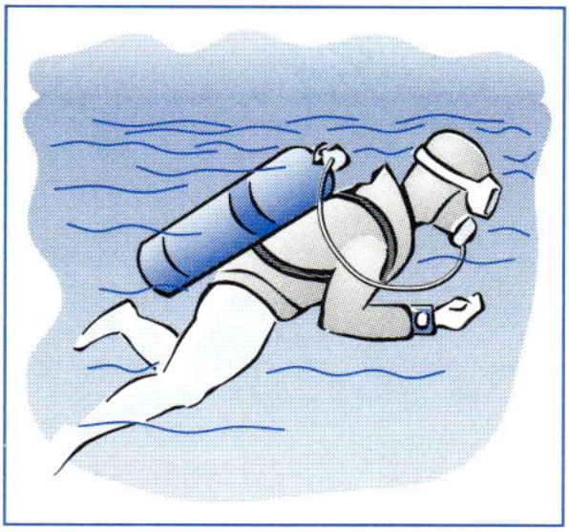

a) He's ....

b) She's ....

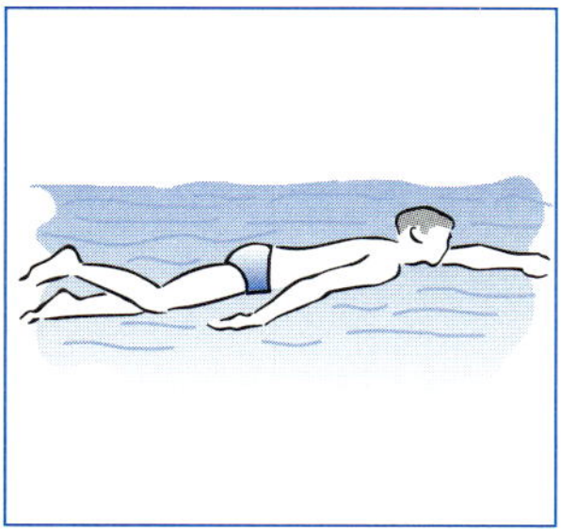

c) He's ....

d) They're ....

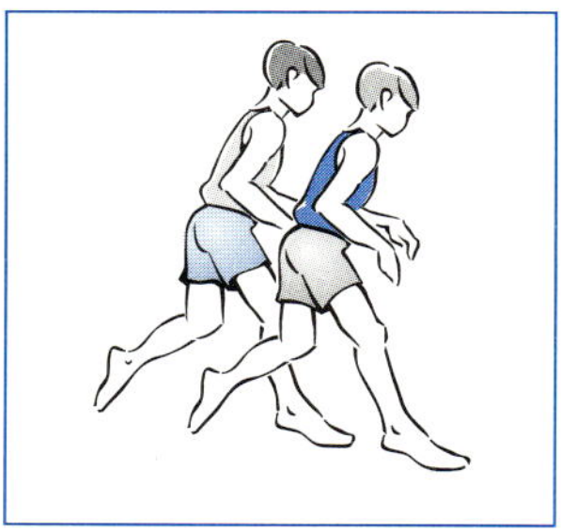

e) They're ....

f) He's ....

g) He's . . . .

h) She's . . . .
the ball

2. Versuchen Sie, die zwölf in diesem Quadrat versteckten Wörter aus dem Sportbereich aufzufinden, indem Sie von oben nach unten und von links nach rechts lesen.

o	q	s	d	f	t	k	j	s	g
r	e	f	e	r	e	e	e	p	s
a	p	o	w	d	a	m	s	e	o
c	g	o	a	l	m	a	t	c	h
k	i	t	d	y	e	r	o	t	n
e	c	b	s	x	r	l	s	a	l
t	r	a	i	n	b	i	c	t	w
f	h	l	l	w	r	p	o	o	l
b	a	l	l	d	h	l	r	r	l
g	a	t	h	l	e	t	e	u	n

3. Vervollständigen Sie die Sätze mit den Wörtern aus dem Kasten.

whistle	stadium	competition
finals	champion	score
race	coach	meda

a) He practised so hard that he actually won the golf ....
b) We've made it into the third round of the competition. If we keep training hard, we'll be in the ....
c) The .... was packed with five thousand spectators.
d) There were five runners in the last ....
e) When he became world ...., he sacked his ....
f) The USA won seven gold ....s in the Olympics.
g) The referee blew his .... after three minutes of injury time.
h) Chelsea managed to .... in the last minute.

Öffentliches Leben 1.4

Staatswesen 1.4.1

Staat und Politik 1.4.1.1

1–2000

1. Vervollständigen Sie die Sätze mit den Wörtern aus dem Kasten.

politics	prince		president
minister	foreigner	border	countries
home	queen		party

a) They walked from Austria into Hungary. They crossed the ....
b) I come from Bombay. India is my ....
c) He doesn't come from this country. He's a ....
d) France and Germany are in Europe. They are European ....

e) He is in the Labour cabinet. He is a government ....
f) She came to the throne when her father died. She's the ....
g) He is at the head of the United States of America. He is the American ....
h) They are the sons of the king. They are ....s.
i) She has always been interested in political affairs. She wants to study ....
j) Britain is governed by Labour. They are the ruling ....

2001–4000

2. Welches Wort passt jeweils nicht?

a) nation, state, politician, colony ....
b) election, flag, vote, majority ....
c) kingdom, elect, crown, royal ....
d) crisis, international, immigrant, foreign ....

3. Wie lautet das Gegenteil?

a) unite ....
b) independent ....
c) immigration ....
d) national ....
e) supporter ....
f) majority ....

4. Welches Wort aus dem Kasten passt jeweils? Achten Sie – wo relevant – auf die Großschreibung.

democracy state
Parliament spy republic
security speech

a) federal –; European –; United –s ....
b) political –; Queen's –; – writer ....
c) Cold War –; East German –; – story ....
d) – measures; – police; – Council ....
e) Irish –; independent –; presidential – ....
f) Houses of –; opening of –; Member of – ....
g) parliamentary –; multiparty –; social – ....

Krieg und Frieden

1.4.1.2

THEMEN

1–4000

1. Fügen Sie das Gegenteil des unterstrichenen Wortes in die Lücke ein.

a) After three years of war, ... returned at last.
b) The troops attacked in the middle of the night, but the villagers .... themselves.
c) After being armed by the government last year, the tribes were .... by the new president.
d) The soldiers were given a warm welcome by the ....
e) In his speech he said that Turkey was a friend, not an ....
f) After a major defeat at the Battle of Balna, the army celebrated their first .... over the enemy.

2001–4000

2. Setzen Sie die Wörter aus dem Kasten in die passende Spalte.

navy	bomb	attack	march
officer	arms	general	sword
gun	occupy	fight	army

troops	*weapons*	*verbs*
....	....	....
....	....	....
....	....	....
....	....	....

3. Wie lautet das Substantiv?

a) arm ....
b) flee ....
c) resist ....
d) defend ....
e) attack ....
f) occupy ....
g) fight ....

1.4.2 *Kirche und Religion*

1–4000

1. Wie heißt es?

a) ....
b) ....
c) ....
d) ....
e) ....
f) ....

2. Vervollständigen Sie die Sätze mit den Wörtern aus dem Kasten.

faith sin service
religion Christmas Easter pray
kneel god believe

a) The Greek ....s had very human characteristics.
b) Moslems .... to Mecca five times a day.
c) We celebrate .... on December 25th.

d) There are two church . . . . s this morning.
e) Do you . . . . in God?
f) Name three great . . . . s of the world.
g) Many people like to . . . . when they pray.
h) He said it's a . . . . to lie.
i) After she lost her family in the earthquake, she lost her Christian . . . .
j) I always eat too many chocolate eggs at . . . .

3. Übersetzen Sie.

a) Der Pfarrer sagt, gute Menschen gehen in den Himmel.
. . . .
b) Glaubst du an die Hölle?
. . . .
c) Sie ist Christin.
. . . .
d) Wir feiern die Geburt Christi zu Weihnachten.
. . . .

Umwelt 1.5

Dorf und Stadt 1.5.1

1–2000

1. Unterstreichen Sie jeweils das richtige Wort.

a) He lives in a tiny *place/city/village* of just 200 people.
b) Canberra is the capital *city/town/centre* of Australia.
c) He's gone to the *city/centre/city centre* to do some shopping.
d) The town hall has a *big place/centre/square* in front of it.
e) They live on a big *castle/tower/farm* in the country.
f) There are 240 steps to the top of the *hall/tower/fence*.
g) The hospital is surrounded by a tall *street/bridge/fence*.

2. STRASSE = *road? / street?* Welche Übersetzung passt?

a) The . . . . to Shilton is very narrow.
b) It's a very busy shopping . . . .
c) I saw three dead foxes on the . . . .
d) There was a lot of glass on the . . . . after the accident.
e) Our neighbourhood has a . . . . party every July.

2001–4000

3. Wie heißt das?

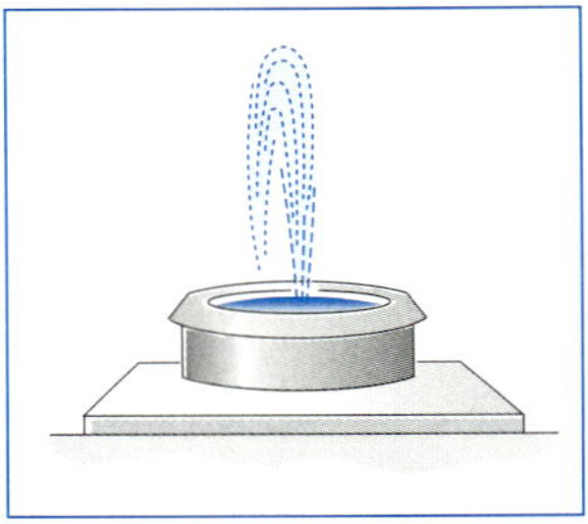

a) ....

b) ....

c) ....

d) ....

e) ....

f) ....

g) ....

h) ....

4. Vervollständigen Sie die Sätze mit Hilfe der Wörter aus dem Kasten.

suburbs	surroundings	local
capital	area	population

a) She lives in an expensive .... Her rent is very high.
b) The .... are very pleasant – we've got fields and woods, and there aren't many cars on the roads.
c) I don't like living in the city centre, I prefer to live in the ....
d) The .... of China is growing very fast.
e) The .... people are very friendly.
f) Is Edinburgh the .... of Scotland, or is it Glasgow?

Landschaft 1.5.2

1–2000

1. Wovon ist hier jeweils die Rede?

a) It's full of trees: ....
b) It lies between two mountains: ....
c) The strip of land next to the sea: ....

d) An area in which you grow potatoes etc.: ....
e) It runs into the sea: ....
f) A large green area in a town: ....
g) An area of water surrounded by land: ....
h) The Alps are made up of these: ....
i) A sandy area next to the sea where people often spend their holidays: ....
j) You walk on this, especially in the country: ....

2. Unterstreichen Sie das richtige Wort.

a) Which is bigger: a spring or a river?
b) Which is higher: a hill or a mountain?
c) Which has more trees: a park or a forest?
d) Which is usually sandy: a beach or a field?
e) Which is surrounded by land on all sides: a river or a lake?
f) What can you enjoy from a mountain top: a field or a view?
g) What do trees grow out of: the ground or a spring?

2001–4000

3. Welches Adjektiv aus dem Kasten verbindet man jeweils am ehesten mit den unten stehenden Substantiven?

strong	deep	dry
green	flat	tropical
hard	rich	steep

a) desert ....
b) meadow ....
c) cliff ....
d) rock ....
e) ditch ....
f) soil ....
g) plain ....
h) current ....
i) island ....

4. Unterstreichen Sie das passende Wort.

a) We skied down a steep *cliff/slope.*
b) They found the drawings in a *cave/source* in southern France.
c) Venice is famous for its *canals/streams.*
d) The *bay/pond* was full of colourful boats and yachts.
e) We found a beach with lovely soft *sand/soil*.

Natur 1.5.3

Allgemeines 1.5.3.1

1–4000

1. Welcher Ausdruck passt jeweils nicht? Streichen Sie ihn durch.

a) ice:	cold, steam, melt
b) fire:	heat, flame, cool
c) flood:	light, wave, water
d) water:	steam, mud, gas
e) air:	gas, steam, shade

2. SCHATTEN = *shadow? / shade?*

Welche Übersetzung passt?

a) I saw the .... of a woman on the wall.
b) I've got very sensitive skin, so I like to stay in the ....
c) This umbrella gives a lot of ....
d) She's frightened of her own ....

1.5.3.2 Tierwelt

1–4000

1. Wie heißen die Tiere?

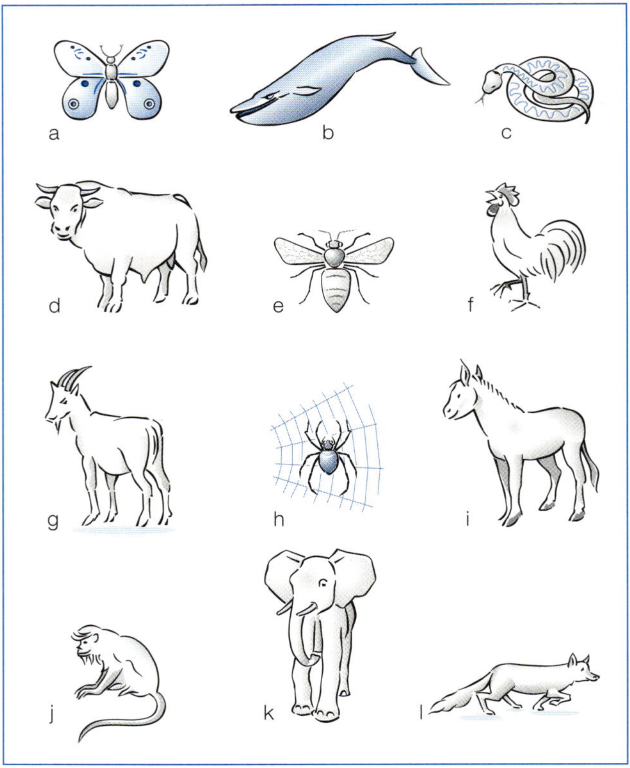

a)	e)	i) ....
b)	f)	j) ....
c)	g)	k) ....
d)	h)	l) ....

2. Welche Tiere gehören in welche Spalte?

lion	turkey	spider
wasp	rabbit	chicken
mosquito	duck	deer
pig	pigeon	beetle

birds	*insects*	*four-legged creatures*
....	....	....
....	....	....
....	....	....
....	....	....

3. Wie lautet die Pluralform?

a) goose ....
b) calf ....
c) mouse ....
d) fish ....
e) sheep ....
f) wolf ....
g) deer ....

4. Welches Tier passt nicht? Streichen Sie es durch.

a) bite:	snake, bee, dog, spider
b) tail:	cow, snake, rat, mouse
c) ride:	horse, donkey, dog, elephant
d) tame:	shark, lamb, rabbit, elephant
e) game:	elephant, lion, deer, fox
f) feathers:	duck, goose, rabbit, turkey
g) wings:	pigeon, mosquito, wasp, whale
h) pets:	dog, shark, cat, rabbit
i) fur:	pig, rabbit, cat, fox
j) track:	elephant, lion, whale, deer

5. Wie lauten die Verbformen? Fügen Sie anschließend die Übersetzung des Verbs hinzu.

			Übersetzung
a) sting	....	....	....
b) bite	....	....	....
c) fly	....	....	....
d) feed	....	....	....
e) breed	....	....	....

1.5.3.3 Pflanzenwelt

1–4000

1. Wie nennt man das?

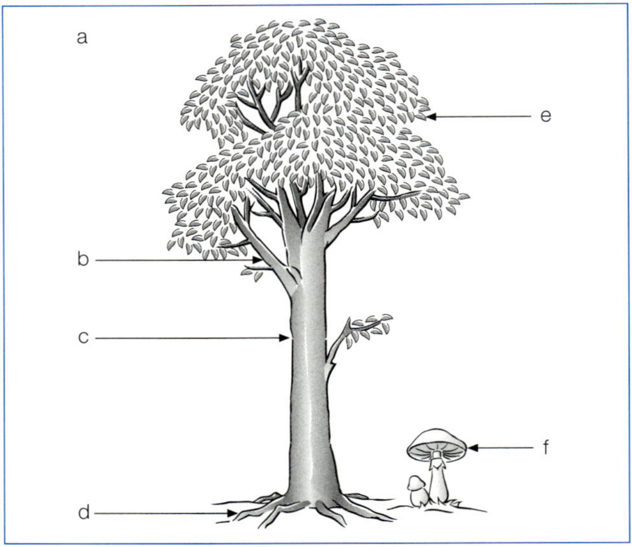

a)	c)	e) ....
b)	d)	f) ....

2. Welche Wörter aus dem Kasten fehlen?

blossom grow seed
weed flower bush hedge
plant fruit grass

Green Fingers

My father is a keen gardener. He likes to grow ....s such as fuchsias, petunias and hyacinths, and he has some lovely rose ....es. He ....s almost everything from ....s, which he puts into small pots and keeps in the greenhouse until they're ready to .... in the garden. We've even got a few .... trees: two apple trees, a plum tree and a cherry tree. The cherry and plum trees look lovely when they're in .... Although my dad loves gardening, he hates cutting the ...., but he doesn't mind trimming the .... that goes all the way round the house. He doesn't like pulling out ....s either, so he gets me to do these things. It's a bit unfair, considering I'm going to be 79 this year.

3. Welches Wort passt jeweils? Unterstreichen Sie es.

a) Wheat is a type of *weed/grain.*
b) Hay is dried *hedge/grass.*
c) Corn is the American word for *maize/grain.*
d) A seed can *sow/grow* into a flower, tree, vegetable or fruit.
e) Blackberries grow on *bushes/hedges.*
f) Many *crops/corns* were destroyed in the tornado.
g) The *harvest/crop* was late this year.

Himmel und Erde

1.5.3.4

1–2000

1. Wie heißen die Himmelsrichtungen?

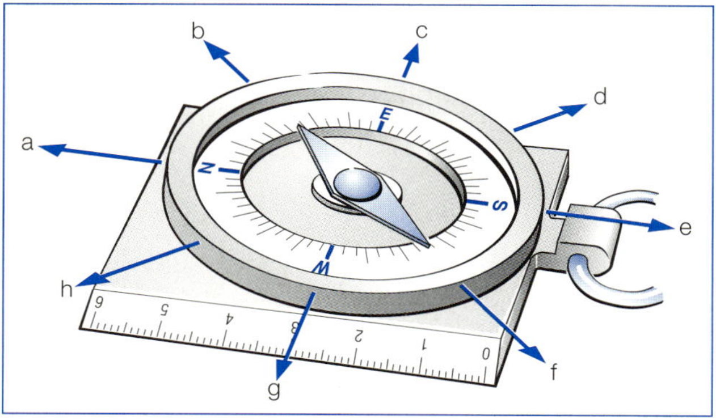

a) ....
b) ....
c) ....
d) ....
e) ....
f) ....
g) ....
h) ....

2. Wie heißen sie?

a) . . . .
b) . . . .
c) . . . .
d) . . . .

1–2000

3. Welches Wort passt jeweils? Unterstreichen Sie es.

a) The satellite circles the *earth/world* twice a day.
b) You could see the stars quite clearly up in the *heaven/sky* last night.
c) Can you show me on the *card/map* where the mountains are?
d) Near our house there is a *lake/sea* surrounded by woods.
e) We're going to sail around the Black *Ocean/Sea* this summer.

1–4000

4. Übersetzen Sie.

a) Der Mond ging um sechs Uhr auf.

. . . .

b) Die Sonne ist schon untergegangen.

. . . .

c) Die Sonne hat jetzt seit fünf Tagen nicht geschienen.

. . . .

d) Der Astronaut war vier Monate im Weltraum.

....

e) Der Himmel ist grau.

....

5. Unterstreichen Sie jeweils das richtige Wort.

a) High *sea/water/tide* is at 10 o'clock.
b) When the sun goes down, we call it a *sundown/set-sun/sunset*.
c) The *poles/rays/shines* of the sun can burn your skin.
d) Where in England do you live? – *The northern/The north/North*.
e) How many stars are there in the *world/space/universe*?

Wetter und Klima 1.5.4

1–4000

1. Welches Wort passt jeweils?

sunshine	weather	frost	storm
climate	temperatures	lightning	rainy

a) .... lovely –; cold –; sunny –; – report
b) .... – day; – weather; – season
c) .... ground –; – on the leaves; – at night
d) .... – at sea; bad –; – clouds
e) .... high –; low –; pleasant –; – around 40° Celsius
f) .... flash of –; be struck by –; thunder and –
g) .... ten hours of –; – and warm temperatures; – followed by rain
h) .... mild –; healthy –; a change in –

2. Wovon ist hier die Rede?

snow	blow	rain	fog
clouds	freezes	mist	
lightning	thunderstorm	frost	

a) They are in the sky and are usually white or grey: ....
b) A storm with thunder and lightning: ....
c) It is wet and falls out of the sky in drops: ....
d) Thick cloud over the ground: ....
e) It usually accompanies thunder: ....
f) It usually comes at night and can kill plants: ....
g) It is white and cold and falls out of the sky: ....
h) The verb that describes what the wind does: ....
i) Water does this at 0° Celsius: ....
j) A light fog: ....

1.5.5 *Umweltprobleme*

1–4000

1. Vervollständigen Sie die Sätze mit Hilfe der Wörter aus dem Kasten.

dump	acid	unleaded
recycle	environment	pollution
smog	catalytic converter	waste

a) The natural world around us is also known as the ....
b) Most cars fill up with .... petrol.
c) .... is a mixture of smoke and fog.
d) What we throw away is called ....
e) To .... something means to use it again.
f) If we make the air, water or soil dirty, we create ....
g) A .... is a place to which we take waste.
h) .... rain kills trees and fish.
i) Modern cars with ....s are cleaner than old cars.

Technik und Materialien 1.6

Energie und Technik 1.6.1

1–2000

1. Welches Wort aus dem Kasten passt jeweils?

engine spring
power machine pump
pipe electricity

a) washing –; ticket –; answering – ....
b) car –; noisy –; diesel – ....
c) water –; electric –; hand – ....
d) water –; burst –; gas – ....
e) – supply; – generator; – bill ....
f) electric –; – supply; – source ....
g) watch –; broken –; mattress – ....

2001–4000

2. Wie heißt das von den Substantiven abgeleitete Adjektiv?

a) mechanics ....
b) sun ....
c) technology .... *oder* ....
d) electricity .... *oder* ....
e) electron ....
f) nucleus ....

3. Welches Wort passt? Unterstreichen Sie es.

a) Have you got *cable/wire* television in your house?
b) This *bar/tube* contains gas which creates the light.
c) We didn't have any *current/electricity* for three days.
d) She's studying *engineering/technique* at Bristol University.
e) Countries with a lot of sun could produce *nuclear/solar* power.
f) To get hot water, just press this *scale/switch.*

1.6.2 *Informationstechnik*

1–4000

1. Vervollständigen Sie die Sätze mit Hilfe der Wörter aus dem Kasten.

floppy disk keyboard software
hardware word processing
hard disk data file
PC printer

a) Printers, monitors and modems are called computer ....
b) Computer programs and games are examples of ....
c) Information in a computer is often called ....
d) You use a .... to type things into a computer.
e) If you want to save data, you must create a ....
f) The part of a computer where data is stored is called the ....
g) If you want to send data to somebody by post, you have to put it on a ....
h) A short name for a personal computer is a ....
j) To type letters, articles or books on a computer you need a .... program.
h) To make a copy of a file on paper, you need a ....

1.6.3 *Materialien*

1–2000

1. Welches Wort passt jeweils nicht? Streichen Sie es durch.

a) jewellery: silver, cotton, gold, metal
b) energy: gas, oil, coal, stone
c) fire: coal, wool, wood, gas
d) diamond: rough, smooth, soft, real
e) paint: wooden, wet, dry, oil
f) textile: woollen, metal, smooth, cotton

2001–4000

2. Versuchen Sie, die zehn in diesem Quadrat versteckten Materialien aufzufinden, indem Sie von oben nach unten und von links nach rechts lesen.

v	p	l	a	s	t	i	c	z	w
r	e	f	e	r	i	r	o	n	g
h	g	t	f	c	n	e	p	w	c
s	t	e	e	l	v	r	p	n	j
i	a	s	x	o	y	p	e	f	d
l	l	e	a	t	h	e	r	e	c
k	s	i	t	h	k	h	k	l	e
d	t	b	c	r	u	b	b	e	r
t	r	u	s	f	s	q	z	a	c
a	k	m	r	d	s	s	w	d	r

3. Welches Wort passt jeweils? Unterstreichen Sie es.

a) In England you find a lot of red-*brick/concrete* houses.
b) Many clothes contain *artificial/material* fibres.
c) Coal is a *liquid/solid* substance.
d) Industry produces a lot of waste *chemicals/mixtures.*
e) We always buy *an artificial/a pure* Christmas tree.
f) Lots of cars use diesel *fuel/mixture.*

1.7 Essen und Trinken

1.7.1 *Allgemeines*

1–4000

1. Welche Wörter aus dem Kasten fehlen?

meal dish hungry thirsty
breakfast lunch dinner
snack swallow drink eat
chew dessert food appetite

Time to eat

When Jeremy gets home in the afternoon, he's always very .... He only has one piece of toast for ...., and he usually doesn't have any .... because he's too busy playing football at that time of day. So as soon as he gets home, he has a big ....: he ....s two bags of crisps and a packet of biscuits. But he ....s everything so fast, without ....ing it properly, that he sometimes gets a stomach-ache. And because of the salted crisps he has eaten, he is so .... that he has to .... about four glasses of milk. When it's time for ...., he's usually too full to have the main .... but he always has room for ...., especially if it's chocolate pudding. But I make him sit at the table during the whole .... When it comes to sweet things and junk ...., he has an .... like a horse. It's a very bad example for the children.

Lebensmittel 1.7.2

Allgemeines 1.7.2.1

1–4000

1. Welche der folgenden Lebensmittel nimmt man üblicherweise als Brotbelag? Schreiben Sie sie ins Sandwich hinein.

soup cake jam cheese
potato ice cream egg salad
rice honey chips sugar
butter flour cereal

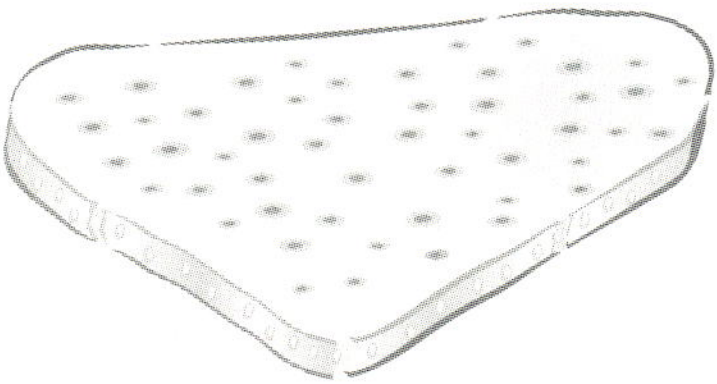

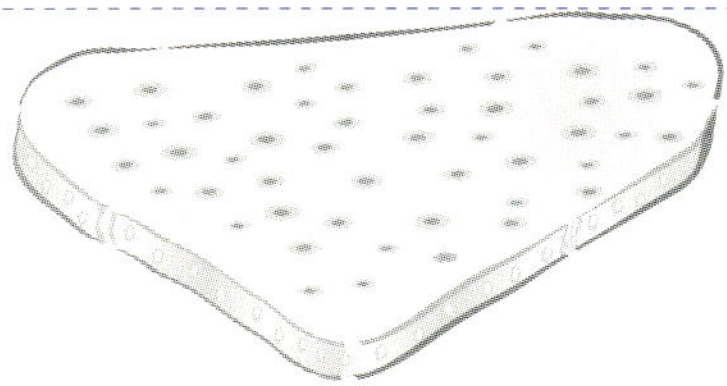

2. Welche Lebensmittel sind üblicherweise süß, welche nicht? Fügen Sie sie in die entsprechende Spalte ein.

	sweet	*not sweet*
chips	....	....
pepper	....	....
sugar	....	....
milk	....	....
bread	....	....
sweets	....	....
egg		
chocolate		
ice cream		
cake		
potato		
jam		

3. Welches Wort passt jeweils nicht? Streichen Sie es durch.

a) cake: flour, salad, butter, eggs
b) breakfast: cereal, egg, soup, milk
c) flour: fat, pie, cake, roll
d) soup: salt, pepper, chocolate, spices
e) milk: butter, cream, cheese, egg

4. Übersetzen Sie.

a) Wir brauchen ein Brot.
....
b) Ich mag Marmelade, aber nicht Orangenmarmelade.
....
c) Magst du Kartoffelchips?
Britisch: ....
Amerikanisch: ....
d) Pommes frites sind voller Fett.
Britisch: ....
Amerikanisch: ....
e) Ich habe nur eine Dose Suppe.
Britisch: ....
Amerikanisch: ....

Fleisch und Fisch 1.7.2.2

1–4000

1. Welche Fleischart stammt jeweils von diesen Tieren?

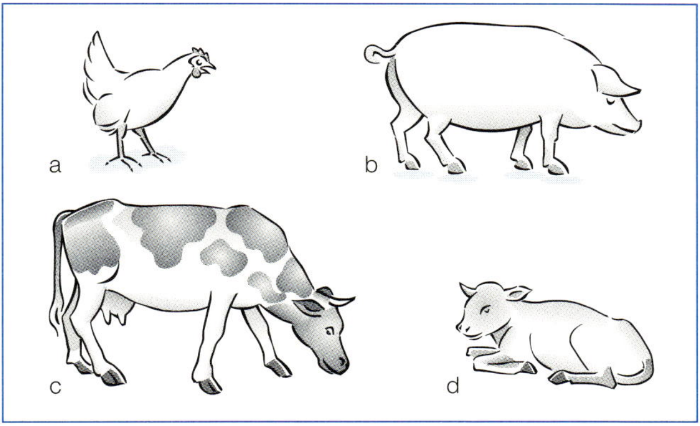

a) . . . .   c) . . . .
b) . . . .   d) . . . .

2. Wie nennt man das?

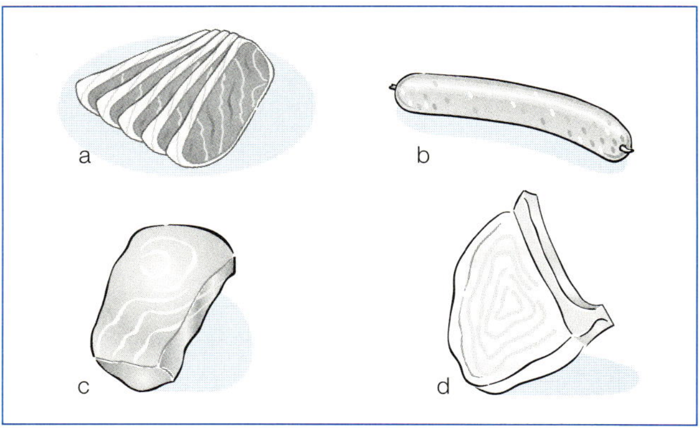

a) . . . .   c) . . . .
b) . . . .   d) . . . .

3. Vervollständigen Sie die Sätze mit Hilfe der Wörter aus dem Kasten.

pork	lean	veal	
tough	bacon	ham	seafood
raw	tender	meat	

a) I don't eat any .... at all. I only eat fish.
b) This is a very fatty chop. Do you have a ....er one?
c) I had difficulty cutting that steak, it was so ....
d) Steak tartare is made with .... beef.
e) This chicken is so .... it almost melts in your mouth.
f) I'm Muslim, so I won't have the .... sandwich or the .... and eggs. I don't eat any kind of .... at all.
g) We don't eat .... because we don't like the way the meat industry treats calves.
h) There are lots of good .... restaurants along the beach that serve excellent fresh fish, crab, shrimps etc.

1.7.2.3 Obst und Gemüse

1–4000

1. Wie nennt man sie?

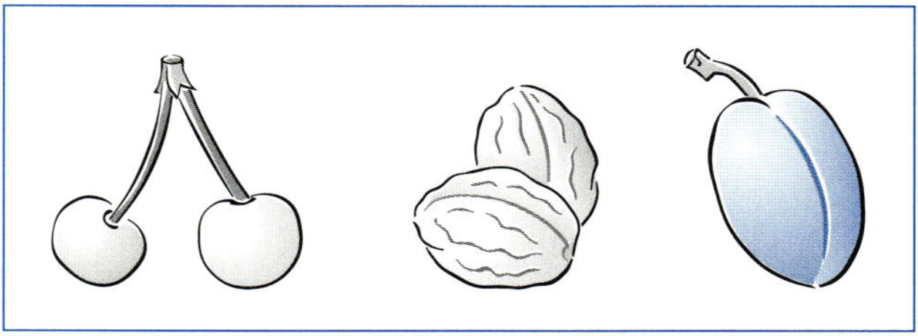

a) .... b) .... c) ....

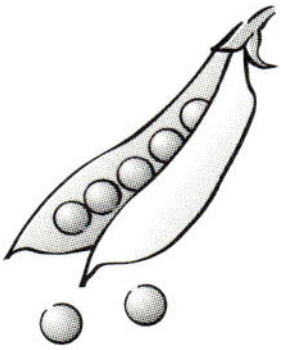
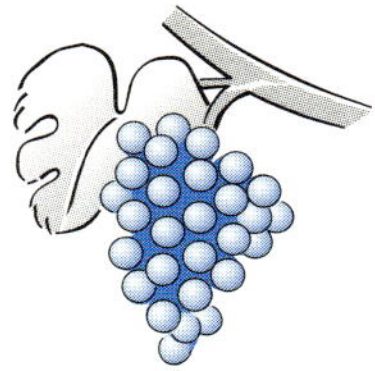
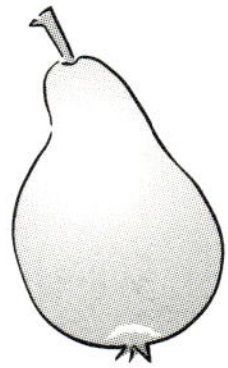

d) ....   e) ....   f) ....

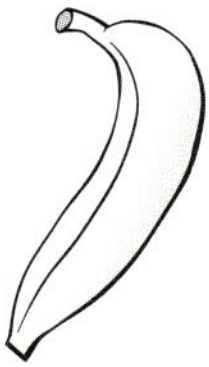
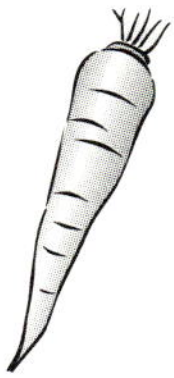

g) ....   h) ....   i) ....

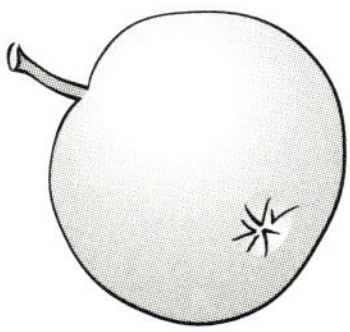
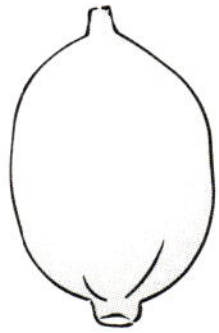
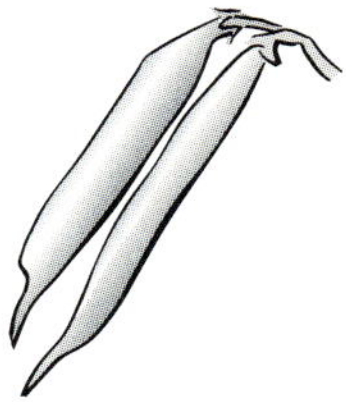

j) ....   k) ....   l) ....

m) ....   n) ....   o) ....

2. Obst oder Gemüse?
Fügen Sie die Wörter in die entsprechende Spalte ein.

	fruit	*vegetables*
tomato	....	....
plum	....	....
pear	....	....
cabbage	....	....
strawberry	....	....
bean	....	....
pea		
cherry		
orange		
onion		
grapes		
carrot		

3. Was gehört in welchen Salat?
Geben Sie die Zutaten in die entsprechende Schüssel (eine der Zutaten gehört in beide).

onion grapes apple herbs
banana carrot cherries
lettuce lemon

fresh salad

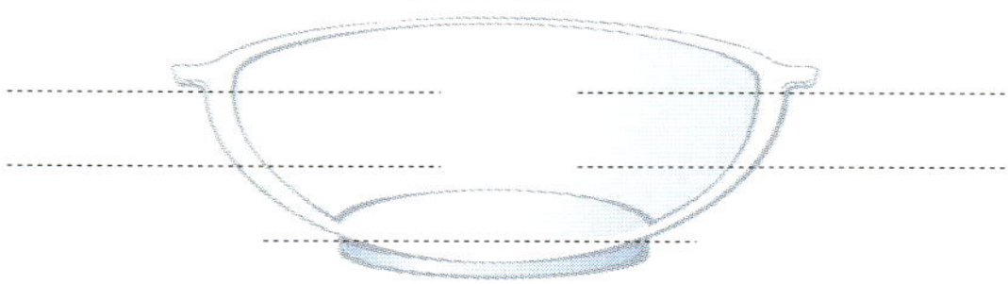

fruit salad

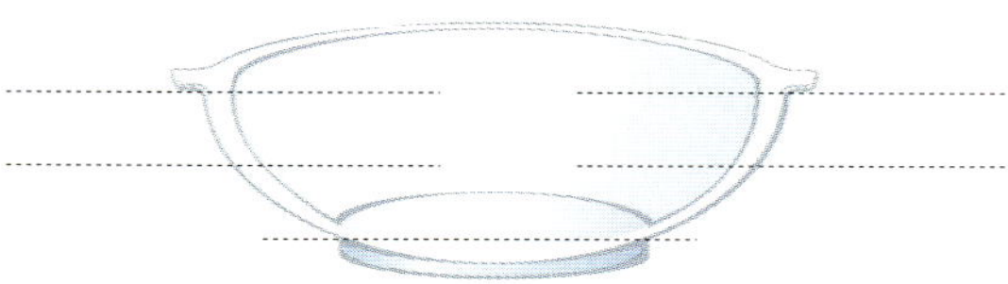

Getränke 1.7.2.4

1–4000

1. Welcher Ausdruck passt jeweils nicht? Unterstreichen Sie ihn.

a) drunk: beer, juice, wine, alcohol
b) wine: dry, soft drink, alcohol, barrel
c) drink: tea, beer, coffee, barrel
d) bottle: juice, tea, beer, wine

2. Welche Wörter fehlen?

a) Some people drink black .... to stay awake.
b) .... is an alcoholic drink made from grapes.
c) A .... is a large container in which wine or beer are kept.
d) If you drink too much alcohol, you will probably get ....
e) I don't like dry wine, I prefer .... wine.
f) Apple juice, tea and coffee are .... drinks.
g) Britain's traditional drink is ....
h) A lot of .... is made from grains.
i) The airline will serve ...., including coffee, tea and sandwiches, in the departure lounge.

Zubereitung der Speisen *1.7.3*

1–4000

1. Welche Verben passen zu den Lebensmitteln?

fry bake boil
roast spread stir

a) cheese: ....
b) soup: ....
c) eggs: ....
d) sausage: ....
e) milk: ....
f) bacon: ....
g) chicken: ....

h) butter: ....
i) cake: ....
j) jam: ....

2. Scheibe oder Tropfen? Fügen Sie die Wörter in die richtige Spalte ein. Ein Wort passt in beide Spalten.

	slice	*drop*
milk	....	....
bread	....	....
cake	....	....
wine	....	....
tomato	....	....
lemon	....	....
beef		
beer		
cheese		
soup		
alcohol		

1.7.4 *Geschirr und Besteck*

1–2000

1. Wie heißt das?

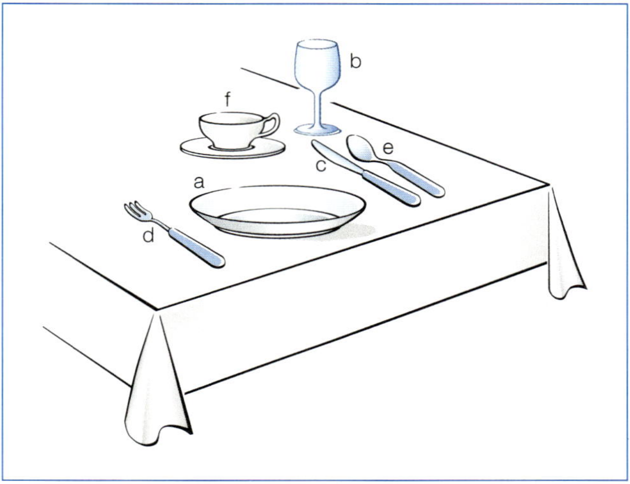

a) . . . .
b) . . . .
c) . . . .
d) . . . .
e) . . . .
f) . . . .

1–4000

2. Vervollständigen Sie die Sätze mit Hilfe der Wörter aus dem Kasten.

opener	handle	bowl	plate
china	pan	cork	
lid	set	fork	saucer
tablecloth	kettle	tray	

a) Don't put your cup on the nice table, put it on the . . . .
b) I've put a big . . . . of milk out for the cats.
c) If you want fried eggs you'll need a frying . . . .
d) He doesn't like knives. He prefers to eat with just a . . . .
e) On Sundays, my mother always puts a clean white . . . . on the table and gets out her best . . . . and glasses.
f) I'll put the . . . . on for some tea.
g) When the soup starts to boil, take the . . . . off.
h) Let's use the smaller . . . . s for bread.
i) I broke one of the Wedgwood saucers, so we don't have a full . . . . any more.
j) I can't carry all these cups – I'd better put them on a . . . .
k) I picked up the coffee pot and the . . . . came off.
l) Dave forgot to bring the bottle . . . ., so we couldn't drink any beer.
m) Malcolm collects wine and champagne . . . . s.

Restaurant 1.7.5

1–4000

1. Welches Wort passt? Unterstreichen Sie es.

a) She works as a *waiter/waitress* in a hotel restaurant.
b) I'd like the *menu/set lunch,* but without the soup.
c) There's a nice *inn/pub* down the road where a lot of young people go to drink.

d) Shall we go to the *bar/snack bar* and have a whisky?
e) Is this a *service/self-service* cafeteria?
f) Can I take your *menu/order* for drinks, please?
g) He earns a lot of money from *orders/tips*.
h) The *serve/service* in this restaurant is very quick.

1.8 Reise und Verkehr

1.8.1 *Reise*

1–2000

1. Vervollständigen Sie die Sätze mit Hilfe der Wörter aus dem Kasten.

passenger	hotel	customs	timetable	
luggage	abroad	leave	travel	
catch	guide	way	stay	run

a) You'd better hurry if you want to .... the coach to Brighton.
b) A policeman showed me the .... to the British Museum.
c) Trains to Glasgow .... every hour.
d) Our local .... in Florence was a German art student.
e) – We're going to Sri Lanka for Christmas.
– How long are you ....ing for?
f) I just want to check the .... to see exactly when her train arrives.
g) He hasn't been .... for over twenty years.
h) We were stopped at .... and had to unpack all our ....
i) Have you ever been to a five-star .... ?
j) Some ....s missed their flight because of the heavy traffic.
k) I like to ...., but I'm afraid of flying.
l) It was such a wonderful holiday, we didn't want to ....

2. Wie lautet das Gegenteil?

a) departure ....
b) catch ....
c) arrive ....

3. Setzen Sie die Verben in die einfache Vergangenheit.

a) He .... (go) all the way to Hungary by car.
b) We .... (stay) in a villa in Tuscany for six weeks.
c) I hope the children .... (catch) the first bus.
d) I .... (miss) the train by a minute.
e) He said the train only .... (run) twice on Sundays.
f) They .... (leave) for the airport at eight o'clock.

2001–4000

4. Welches Wort passt?

accommodation tourist luggage

a) sightseeing, visa, tour, map: ....
b) tent, youth hostel, bed and breakfast: ....
c) suitcase, pack, bag: ....

5. Welche Verben passen in diese Sätze? Die jeweilige Anzahl wird in Klammern angegeben.

declare check in land pick up pack

a) How many pieces of luggage did you ....? (3)
b) I forgot to .... the extra bottle of whisky. (3)
c) What time do we .... at Heathrow? (2)

1–4000

6. Welches Wort passt nicht? Streichen Sie es durch.

a) Did you enjoy your *travel/trip/stay*?
b) They just *caught/missed/checked in* the bus.
c) We're looking for a *youth hostel/camping/bed and breakfast.*
d) Have you ever *travelled/started/gone* abroad?
e) I really enjoyed our bicycle *tour/trip/sightseeing.*

1.8.2 *Verkehr*

1.8.2.1 Straßenverkehr

1.8.2.1.1 *Allgemein*

1–2000

1. Welche Substantive passen jeweils zu den Verben?

car road motorcycle bus
path bicycle river bridge

a) cross: ....
b) ride: ....
c) drive: ....

1–4000

2. Welches Wort aus der rechten Spalte passt jeweils zur Definition?

a) Somebody who is walking in the street:	petrol
b) A road on which you can drive fast:	bend
c) Where two roads meet and form a cross:	traffic
d) The person in control of a car:	garage
e) To leave a car at the side of the road:	pedestrian
f) You fill a car up with this:	driver
g) A part of the road which isn't straight:	park
h) Cars, buses etc. on the road:	crossroads
i) Where you take a car to be repaired:	motorway

3. Vervollständigen Sie die Sätze mit Hilfe der Wörter aus dem Kasten.

park	petrol	stop	lights	limit
hour	driving	helmet	belt	rush

a) I think dogs who travel in cars should wear seat ....s.
b) She was driving over the speed ....
c) I hate cycling in the .... hour.
d) He was 50 when he got his .... licence.
e) There was a long queue at the .... station.
f) That car just went through the traffic .... at red!
g) Was he wearing a crash .... when the accident happened?
h) The car .... was completely full.
i) She had to wait at the bus .... for an hour before a bus came.

4. Wie lauten die amerikanischen Entsprechungen?

a) motorway ....
b) driving licence ....
c) petrol ....
d) car park ....
e) filling station ....

Fahrzeuge 1.8.2.1.2

1–4000

1. Welches Fahrzeug steckt im jeweiligen Buchstabensalat?

a) cibylce ....
b) royrl ....
c) arc ....
d) ravacan ....
e) rotomlycce ....
f) ubs ....
g) ructk ....
h) mart ....
i) axti ....

2. Worum geht es hier?

a) It has two wheels and an engine: . . . .
b) You can order one to take you to the station: . . . .
c) It is pulled by a car and used for carrying loads: . . . .
d) Another name for a bicycle: . . . .
e) A general name for anything on wheels: . . . .
f) A bus for long journeys: . . . .
g) Lorries have at least four, sometimes 20 or more: . . . .
h) It is pulled by a car and used for holidays: . . . .

1.8.2.2 Eisenbahn

1–4000

1. Welche Wörter aus dem Kasten fehlen?

car	carriage	platform	waiting	
train (2x)	rail	underground	connection	
guard	office	station	change	compartment

The Joys of Travelling

I hate travelling to work by . . . . every day because you can't see anything out of the window. But I love . . . . travel. Last weekend I took the . . . . to see my cousin in Cornwall. After queuing at the ticket . . . . for ten minutes, I still had time to sit in the . . . . room and read my newspaper before slowly wandering to . . . . 6. I was looking for . . . . number 121, as I had reserved a seat. My seat was in a nice, big, light . . . . with large windows. The train left fifteen minutes late, and as soon as it moved out of the . . . . I went to the dining . . . . for a snack. I knew I had to . . . . at Newton Abbot, but I wasn't sure if I would catch my . . . . because the train was running late. When I asked the . . . . about it, he told me the train wasn't going to Newton Abbot, it was on its way to Bristol! I had to get off at the next stop, go back to London and start again. It's a good thing I enjoy travelling by . . . .!

Flugzeug 1.8.2.3

1–4000

1. Welches Wort passt am besten? Unterstreichen Sie es.

a) There are at least five *wings/flights* a day.
b) The nearest *airline/airport* is twenty miles away.
c) One of the aircraft's *wings/planes* broke off.
d) They're checking all the engines on Jumbo *airlines/jets.*
e) What time is the plane scheduled to *crash/take off?*
f) The aircraft is on the runway ready for *flight/takeoff.*

Schiff 1.8.2.4

1–4000

1. Vervollständigen Sie die Sätze mit Hilfe der Wörter aus dem Kasten.

captain	sailor	boat	ship
ferry	voyage	port	drown
crossing	wreck	cruise	sail

a) We went on a Mediterranean cruise on a large .... carrying 1,200 passengers.
b) The harbour looked very picturesque with its colourful fishing ....s.
c) The ship's .... invited us to sit at his table for dinner.
d) The ....s had to run all the way back to the ship before it sailed.
e) The Ostende to Dover .... was very calm, but I was still seasick.
f) What time does the ferry ....?
g) My parents are saving up for a round-the-world ....
h) The archaeologists showed us some of the objects they had brought up from the ....
i) Several passengers and crew ....ed in the accident.
j) Hamburg is still a busy ....

k) Many sailors died during the . . . . s of discovery in the 15th and 16th centuries.
l) We don't take the . . . . to France any more: we always travel through the Channel Tunnel.

1.8.2.5 Raumfahrt

1–4000

1. Welches Wort passt zu welcher Beschreibung?

astronaut rocket space shuttle
spacecraft space flight satellite

a) It is used to transmit television programmes: . . . .
b) You need this to launch a spacecraft: . . . .
c) Ulf Merbold is a famous German one: . . . .
d) People are sent into space in this: . . . .
e) The first manned one was in 1961: . . . .
f) It is built to travel between space and the earth several times: . . . .

1.9 Länder und Völker

1.9.1 *Länder*

1–4000

1. Wie lauten die fünf Erdteile?

a) A _ _ a
b) A _ r i c _
c) E _ r _ _ e
d) A u _ _ r _ l i _
e) A m _ _ i c _

2. Füllen Sie die Lücken.

a) USA is short for the . . . . of America.
b) England and Wales are part of . . . .
c) Bavaria is part of the Federal Republic of . . . .
d) Another name for Holland: the . . . .
e) A country in southeastern Europe that has the same name as a big bird: . . . .
f) A British country that sounds like large animals living in the sea: . . . .

g) A European country without a coast that is famous for its cheese: ....
h) A south European country that is shaped like a boot: ....
i) A country in eastern Europe that sounds as if it needs some food: ....
j) Three Scandinavian countries: N.........., D.......... and S..........
k) The Asian country with the highest number of people in the world: ....
l) A European country in which French and Flemish are spoken: ....
m) Its capital is Madrid: ....
n) Its capital is Athens: ....

3. Übersetzen Sie.

a) Die USA sind sehr interessant.
....
b) Wir fliegen in die Schweiz.
....
c) Ich komme aus Schottland.
....
d) Sie will nach Polen fahren.
....
e) Wir reisen nach der Türkei.
....
f) Frankreich ist in der Europäischen Union.
....

Bewohner 1.9.2

1–4000

1. Füllen Sie die Lücken mit den entsprechenden Substantiven, z. B. *We're from Norway. We're <u>Norwegians.</u>*

a) We're from Europe. We're ....
b) He's from Ireland. He's an ....
c) Those men are from France. They're ....
d) The children are from Germany. They're ....
e) My sister-in-law is from Italy. She's an ....
f) My aunts are from the Netherlands. They're ....
g) Her boyfriend is from Greece. He's a ....

h) The people of China have more bicycles than cars. Most of the .... are cyclists.
i) The people of Britain drink a lot of tea. The .... are tea-drinkers.
j) She's from England. She's an ....
k) Her friends are from Africa. They're ....
l) The lady in the kimono is from Japan. She's a ....
m) The author is from India. He's an ....
n) The people of the Netherlands learn languages easily. The .... are good at languages.
o) The people of Switzerland like climbing mountains. The .... are mountain-climbers.
p) My Uncle George is from Scotland. He's a ....

1.9.3 *Sprachen und Nationalitäten*

1–4000

1. Übersetzen Sie die deutschen Wörter in Klammern.

a) I love .... *(Schweizer)* chocolate.
b) I'm learning .... *(Italienisch)* before we go on holiday to Florence.
c) You're from Germany and I'm from France, so we're both .... *(europäisch).*
d) I can only speak a little bit of .... *(Russisch).*
e) He has an .... *(österreichischen)* accent. He comes from Graz.
f) His mother is .... *(englisch)* and his father is .... *(schottisch),* so he's .... *(britisch).*
g) I learnt .... *(Französisch)* and .... *(Spanisch)* at school, but I've forgotten everything.
h) She's from Cyprus, but I don't know if she's a .... *(griechisch)* or .... *(türkisch)* Cypriot.
i) They're from Brazil, so they speak .... *(Portugiesisch).*
j) I've learnt 100 .... *(japanische)* characters already.
k) .... *(Holländisch)* is in some ways similar to German.

Zeit 2.1

Jahresablauf 2.1.1

1–2000

1. Welche Jahreszeiten werden in den Zeichnungen dargestellt?

a) ....

b) ....

c) ....

d) ....

2. Fügen Sie die fehlenden Wörter ein.

a) There are 24 hours in a . . . .
b) There are 12 months in a . . . .
c) There are seven days in a . . . .
d) There are between 28 and 31 days in a . . . .
e) A year has 52 . . . .
f) A week has seven . . . .
g) A month has about four . . . .
h) A year has twelve . . . . and usually 365 . . . .

1–4000

3. Wie könnte man es anders ausdrücken?

a) The newspaper comes out every day. It's a . . . . newspaper.
b) The magazine comes out once a week. It's a . . . . magazine.
c) He comes to see us once a month. He visits us on a . . . . basis.
d) I work from Monday to Friday. I only work on . . . .
e) He always works on Saturday and Sunday. He works at the . . . .
f) Autumn is my favourite time of the year. Autumn is the . . . . I like best.
g) Are you going away in July or August? Are you going on . . . . this summer?
h) Will you be having a party on December 31st? Are you going to celebrate . . . . ?

4. Wie lautet die fehlende Präposition?

a) Where are you going . . . . holiday?
b) What's the weather like . . . . spring?
c) I'm not doing anything . . . . the weekend.
d) How many hours of work do you do . . . . a day?
e) We're going to have a quiet celebration . . . . New Year's Eve.
f) We don't go anywhere . . . . the week.
g) It's cheaper to go . . . . a weekday.

Monatsnamen 2.1.2

1. Versuchen Sie, die Monate im Jahr zu entwirren. Bringen Sie sie dann in die richtige Reihenfolge.

a) braurefy ....
b) botcore ....
c) yluj ....
d) tugsua ....
e) metperbes ....
f) mercedeb ....
g) harmc ....
h) rilpa ....
i) neju ....
j) bermoven ....
k) yam ....
l) rajanuy ....

....
....
....
....

Wochentage 2.1.3

1. Von welchen Wochentagen ist hier die Rede?

a) It's the first day of the week: ....
b) It's the day on which some people go to church: ....
c) It's the day after Monday: ....
d) It's named after the god of thunder: ....
e) It comes at the end of the week: ....
f) It's the first day of the weekend: ....
g) It's right in the middle of the week: ....

2.1.4 *Tageszeit*

1–4000

1. Wie nennt man die Tageszeiten *(morning, midnight usw.)*?

a) .... b) .... c) ....

d) .... e) .... f) ....

g) .... h) .... i) ....

Uhrzeit

2.1.5

1–2000

1. Wie viel Uhr ist es?
Schreiben Sie die Uhrzeiten vollständig aus.

a) .... b) .... c) ....

d) .... e) .... f) ....

2. Übersetzen Sie.

a) Um wie viel Uhr kommst du?

....

b) Ich komme um drei.

....

c) – Wie lange ist der Film?
– Zwei Stunden.

....

d) Du hast dreißig Sekunden.

....

e) Es ist sechs Uhr.

....

2.1.6 *Andere Zeitbegriffe*

2.1.6.1 Heute, gestern und morgen

1–2000

1. Unterstreichen Sie jeweils das richtige Wort.

a) What did you do *now/tomorrow/today*?
b) Just a *while/moment/time*!
c) He's the *present/near/now* chancellor.
d) It's going to happen in the near *present/century/future*.
e) It happened two days *ago/now/past*.

2. *Past, present* oder *future*? Geben Sie jeweils die richtige Zeitdimension an.

a) It was invented a long time ago. ....
b) We're going to Spain next month. ....
c) He's studying at the University of Cordoba. ....
d) It's a nice day today. ....
e) When are you moving house? ....
f) He rang up while you were out. ....
g) Do it now! ....
h) She gets back tomorrow. ....
i) What day is the 7th of November? ....

**3. WÄHREND = *while?/during?*
Unterstreichen Sie die Übersetzung, die stimmt.**

a) He rang me up *while/during* dinner.
b) I like to listen to the radio *while/during* I work.
c) What are you doing *while/during* the summer?
d) He always calls *while/during* we're out.
e) It gets quite noisy *while/during* the night.

1–4000

**4. Nehmen wir an, heute sei Mittwoch.
Fügen Sie jeweils den entsprechenden Zeitbegriff ein (z. B. *yesterday* usw.).**

a) It is Wednesday ....
b) .... was Tuesday.
c) .... it will be Thursday.

d) Friday is .... *(übermorgen)*.
e) Monday was .... *(vorgestern)*.
f) Saturday was four ....
g) Wednesday evening is ....
h) .... was Tuesday evening.

5. Vervollständigen Sie die Sätze mit Hilfe der Wörter aus dem Kasten.

when	in	then	period
nowadays	this	date	meanwhile

a) What's the .... today?
b) They got married .... 1988.
c) How old were you ....?
d) She used to be very lazy. .... she's a workaholic.
e) .... I last saw them, they were living in Cardiff.
f) What time did you get up .... morning?
g) We studied medicine together. .... he's become a well-known heart surgeon.
h) I think the Renaissance is the most interesting .... in art.

Dauer 2.1.6.2

1–2000

1. SEIT = *for? / since?*

Fügen Sie die richtige Übersetzung ein.

a) I've been here .... five o'clock.
b) I've been here .... three hours.
c) He's been awake .... I got back from town.
d) I've had this headache .... yesterday.
e) I've been taking these tablets .... a fortnight.

1–4000

2. Wie könnte man es anders ausdrücken?

a) He'll be back soon. He'll be back in a ....
b) I'll see you in two weeks. I'll see you in a ....

c) How long is the swimming pool? What is the ....
of the swimming pool?
d) We'll be here until Friday. We'll be here .... two days.
e) I will never stop loving you. I will love you ....
f) They all stop work at half past four. They all work .... half past four.
g) When I got back, he hadn't gone to bed. He was .... up when I got back.

2.1.6.3 Häufigkeit

1–4000

1. Kreuzen Sie jeweils das falsche Kästchen an.

a) – Do you ever go swimming?
- ☐ – Sometimes.
- ☐ – Rarely.
- ☐ – Frequent.

b) I
- ☐ always
- ☐ ever
- ☐ seldom cook for myself.

c) I've
- ☐ always
- ☐ never
- ☐ often met him.

2. Ordnen Sie diese Ausdrücke nach der Häufigkeit und fangen Sie bei der geringsten an.

sometimes rarely always
often never

....

Früher und später 2.1.6.4

1–2000

1. Welcher Ausdruck passt jeweils in alle drei Lücken? Haken Sie das entsprechende Kästchen ab.

a) the guests are here –; have you done it –?; I'm – hungry
☐ just ☐ then ☐ already
b) I'll be back –; how – are we eating?; it'll be dark –
☐ soon ☐ later ☐ after
c) here he is –; you've combed you hair –!; I've done it –
☐ at once ☐ at last ☐ last
d) the programme started –; she's always –; we're right –
☐ early ☐ on time ☐ in time
e) let's do this –; he was – home again; which word comes –?
☐ at first ☐ first ☐ at once
f) it can wait till –; see you –; I'll do it –
☐ late ☐ last ☐ later
g) I'll eat it –; he's coming –; we went to a disco –
☐ afterwards ☐ before ☐ soon
h) I jog – breakfast; he went home – work; what comes – this?
☐ afterwards ☐ after ☐ then
i) it's – eight o'clock; is it – Tuesday?; it's – the third
☐ first ☐ then ☐ only
j) she's – come; I've – eaten; they're – leaving
☐ just ☐ early ☐ soon
k) what did you do –?; think – you speak; I've seen you –
☐ already ☐ first ☐ before

2. Vervollständigen Sie die Übersetzungen mit Hilfe der Ausdrücke im Kasten.

at once · at last · later · before · already · late · afterwards · soon · on time · in time · first · early · only · then

a) *Bis bald!* See you . . . .
b) *Bis später!* See you . . . .

c) *Endlich bist du da!*	You're here ....
d) *Was sagte er dann?*	What did he say ....?
e) *Es ist erst drei.*	It's .... three.
f) *Pünktlich wie immer!*	.........., as always.
g) *Gerade noch rechtzeitig!*	Just ....
h) *Schon müde?*	Tired ....?
i) *Das machen wir danach.*	We'll do it ....
j) *Du bist spät.*	You're ....
k) *Ich esse zuerst.*	I'll eat ....
l) *Ich mache es sofort.*	I'll do it ....
m) *Warst du schon mal hier?*	Have you been here ....?
n) *Er war 1 Stunde zu früh.*	He was an hour ....

2001–4000

3. Wie könnte man es anders ausdrücken? Der erste Buchstabe des fehlenden Wortes wird jeweils als Hilfe angegeben.

a) Have you seen any movies lately? Have you been to the cinema r..........?
b) I'm never on time. I'm not a p.......... person.
c) That was the last in the series. That was the f.......... episode.
d) They rang her up at once. They called her i..........
e) He's passed his exams at last. He's f.......... got through his exams.
f) My first reaction was to say no. A.......... .... I said no.
g) Is she here already? Has she arrived y..........?

2.1.7 *Zeitlicher Ablauf*

1–2000

1. Setzen Sie das eingeklammerte Verb in die einfache Vergangenheit.

a) Everyone .... (keep) very quiet during last night's performance.
b) It suddenly .... (begin) to rain.
c) He .... (become) Prime Minister in 1997.
d) The hot weather .... (go on) for three weeks.
e) After three hours he .... (get) very impatient.

2. Welche Dialoghälften aus der linken und rechten Spalte passen zusammen?

a) Is dinner ready yet?	t) Well finish it, and then show it to me.
b) Could you say that again, please?	u) You shouldn't have stopped.
c) Shall I continue playing this piece?	v) Yes, I'm afraid the concert is over.
d) How many times have you been to the opera?	w) No, I haven't even finished peeling the potatoes.
e) I've just started typing a letter.	x) No, her condition hasn't changed since last week.
f) Is she making any progress?	y) I've already repeated it once.
g) Is that the end?	z) Only twice.

a) .... c) .... e) .... g) ....
b) .... d) .... f) ....

2001–4000

3. Welches Wort passt? Unterstreichen Sie es.

a) We're sorry for the *delay/interrupt,* which is due to heavy rain.
b) Please *remain/take place* in your seats.
c) They *delayed/interrupted* the programme during the most exciting moment.
d) A well-known historian wrote the *beginning/introduction* to the book.
e) How long is this lovely weather going to *keep/last?*
f) This situation will *remain/be permanent* for at least five years.
g) We're now in the final *stadium/stage* of the project.
h) The war *lasted/remained* seven years.
i) They are making great progress in the *developing/development* of medical treatment.
j) This is a very *actual/up-to-date* book on English.

2.2 Raum

2.2.1 *Räumliche Begriffe*

1–2000

1. Wie lautet das Gegenteil des unterstrichenen Wortes?

a) – Is it here? – No, it's over ....
b) – Do we fly above 10,000 metres? – No, we stay .... that level.
c) There are 230 pupils in the upper school, and 340 in the .... school.
d) – Is it very near? – No, it's quite ....
e) I've looked .... for my glasses, but they're nowhere to be found.
f) – Is Paul in? – No, he's .... playing football.
g) The passage is very ...., and the car's too wide to get through.
h) – Is that mountain as high as the Matterhorn? – No, it's ....er.
i) Take the first road right, then the second road ....
j) All you people at the back please come to the ....
k) What goes up has to come ....
l) All the dogs jumped over the fence, but Shane went .... it.

2. Fügen Sie die richtige Präposition ein.

a) She's sitting .... the wall.

b) She's pushing .... the wall.

c) She's throwing a ball
. . . . the wall.

d) She's standing
. . . . the wall.

e) She's hiding
. . . . the wall.

f) She's standing
. . . . the wall.

ALLGEMEINES

3. Vervollständigen Sie die Sätze mit den Ausdrücken aus dem Kasten.

among	to	where	somewhere
opposite		place	side
anywhere	flat	straight	distance
deep		room	surface
	at	away	

a) Don't go into the . . . . end – you can't swim properly yet!
b) Just write on one . . . . of the page, please.
c) He was so drunk he couldn't walk in a . . . . line.
d) This looks like a nice . . . . for a picnic.
e) How far is it . . . . your office?

f) .... do you live?
g) We live .... our school. We just have to cross the road and we're there.
h) There are a lot of Africans .... the students.
i) It's a very ...., uninteresting desert.
j) We covered a .... of 400 miles in six hours.
k) There's only .... for six people at the table.
l) The .... of the lake was very calm.
m) Aren't you going .... over Easter?
n) Our grandparents live just three miles ....
o) I'll meet you .... Harry's Bar just after seven.
p) Well, your socks must be ....

4. NÄCHST- = *nearest? / next?*

Fügen Sie die richtige Übersetzung ein.

a) Turn left at the .... traffic lights.
b) Can you tell me where the .... post office is from here?
c) The .... hospital to our house is 20 miles away.
d) Mr Warren's office is on the .... floor.
e) Get off at the .... stop and take the number 59 bus.
f) Where's the .... toilet?

2001–4000

5. Unterstreichen Sie jeweils den richtigen Ausdruck.

a) The accident happened at this *space/position/spot.*
b) What *height/depth/width* do you dive to?
c) We live in a very *inner/central/inside* position.
d) I went *outer/aside/outside* to see how cold it was.
e) My flat is right *on top/on top of/at the top of* the building.
f) The page number is *below/at the bottom of/at the bottom* the screen.
g) The dog walked *all over/throughout/all throughout* my clean floor.

Bewegung und Ruhe 2.2.2

1–2000

1. Welches Verb aus dem Kasten passt jeweils?

turn fall sink
jump rise
sit move lie

a) horse, person, frog: ....
b) hot air, sun, moon: ....
c) ship, water level, stone: ....
d) currency, leaves, rain: ....
e) driver, class, dog: ....
f) person, train, eyes: ....
g) wheel, carousel, earth: ....
h) baby, patient, carpet: ....

2. Welches Verb ist richtig? Unterstreichen Sie es.

a) The sun *rose/raised* at half past six this morning.
b) They *rose/raised* the stage for the concert.
c) The balloon has *rose/risen* to a height of 1,000 metres.
d) I *lay/lied* down for half an hour and then I started cooking.
e) Hugo *lay/laid* the baby on the sofa.
f) She was *laying/lying* in bed when I got home.

2001–4000

3. Welches Substantiv passt jeweils nicht? Streichen Sie es durch.

a) roll: ball, house, stone, egg
b) flow: river, aircraft, traffic, tears
c) float: ship, tree, swimmer, rock

d) slip: beer, tyres, person, shoe
e) creep: tiger, snake, fish, fox
f) hang: leaves, clothes, meat, earth
g) rock: baby, bicycle, boat, chair

4. Welches Wort passt? Unterstreichen Sie es.

a) He was crossing the bridge when he lost his *balance/ presence.*
b) The gondolas *floated/flowed* past on the canal.
c) We felt the *rock/shock* of the explosion in our house.
d) I *slipped/crept* on a banana skin and broke my ankle.
e) They *pushed/rocked* their way to the front of the queue.
f) There has been a sharp *rise/shock* in the value of the deutschmark.
g) There was a sudden *movement/rise* behind the curtain, and Mr Grant appeared dressed as Father Christmas.

2.2.3 *Schnell und langsam*

1–4000

1. Vervollständigen Sie die Ausdrücke.

a) Don't rush. We're not in a h _ _ _ y.
b) He slowed down to let me _ _ e r t _ k _.
c) I _ _ n all the way to the shop, but it was already closed.
d) I did my homework as _ a s _ as I could.
e) We took the _ l _ w train to Bergen and enjoyed the journey very much.
f) What is the world land _ p e _ _ record?
g) I'll be as _ u i _ _ as I can.
h) _ u r _ _ up! We haven't got much time!
i) We _ u s h _ _ outside to see the balloon, but it had disappeared behind the trees.

Richtung 2.2.4

1–4000

1. Fügen Sie die richtige Präposition bzw. das richtige Adverb ein.

a) The man is getting .... the bus.

b) The woman is getting .... of the car.

c) The children are walking .... the river.

d) The children are dancing .... the girl.

e) The car is going ....

f) The boat is going .... the river.

g) The woman is going .... a shop.

h) The child is running .... its mother.

i) The man is walking .... the door.

j) The soldier is stepping ....

2. Wie könnte man es anders ausdrücken?

a) Is this the right way to Calais? Is this the right .... for Calais?
b) They continued walking for a mile. They walked .... for a mile.
c) We could see the Tower of London as the aeroplane got closer to the airport. We could see the Tower as the aeroplane .... the airport.
d) Does this train go to Birmingham? Is this the train .... Birmingham?
e) My home is in Denmark. I come .... Denmark.
f) I saw Timothy running down the street. I saw him running .... the street.
g) The car drove away very fast. The car drove .... very fast.
h) We swam to the other side of the lake. We swam .... the lake.

Kommen und Gehen 2.2.5

1–2000

1. Welches Verb aus dem Kasten fehlt jeweils? Setzen Sie es in der richtigen Zeitform ein.

stop	disappear	pass	enter
go	wander	return	
settle	leave	arrive	reach
appear	get	walk	

a) Are you coming or .... ?
b) As I was walking down the High Street, Mandy .... me in her new sports car.
c) They found the little girl .... around in the woods alone.
d) The last train .... half an hour ago.
e) How long will it take us to .... there?
f) When did she last .... on stage?
g) He doesn't say "Come in!", he says "..........!", which is a bit formal.
h) After a trek of 14 days, they .... Ecuador.
i) He wants to move to Canada with his family and .... there.
j) Does the London to Edinburgh train .... at Newcastle?
k) Harry could .... before he could talk.
l) We .... just before Ken left.
m) Their cat has .... They haven't seen him for three days.
n) The astronauts are due to .... to earth in four weeks.

2.3 Menge und Maß

2.3.1 *Mengenbegriffe*

1–2000

1. Vervollständigen Sie die Ausdrücke.

a) a .... eggs

b) a .... of the pizza

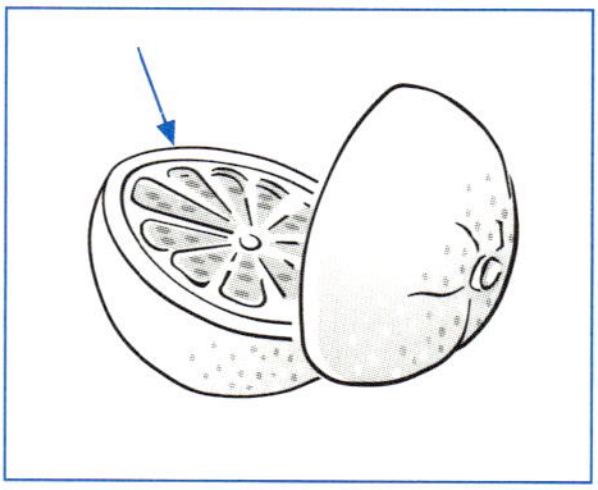

c) .... an orange

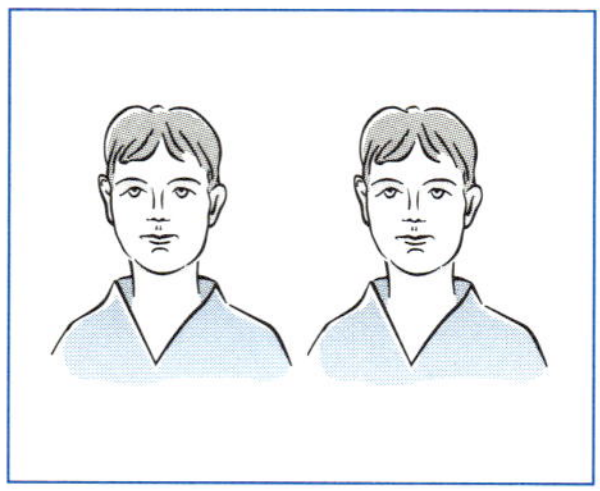

d) .... boys are the same

e) a .... cars

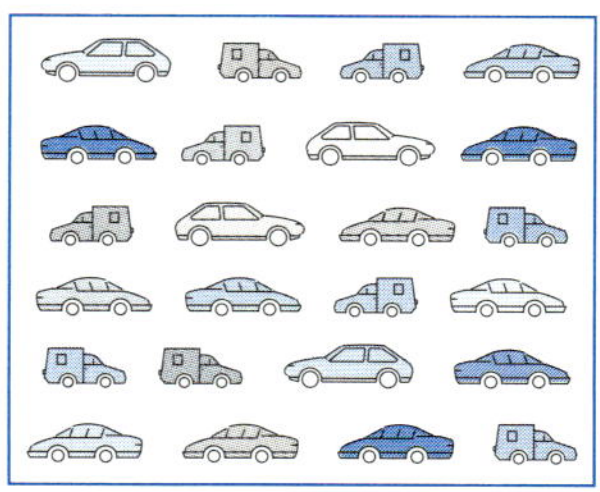

f) a .... of cars

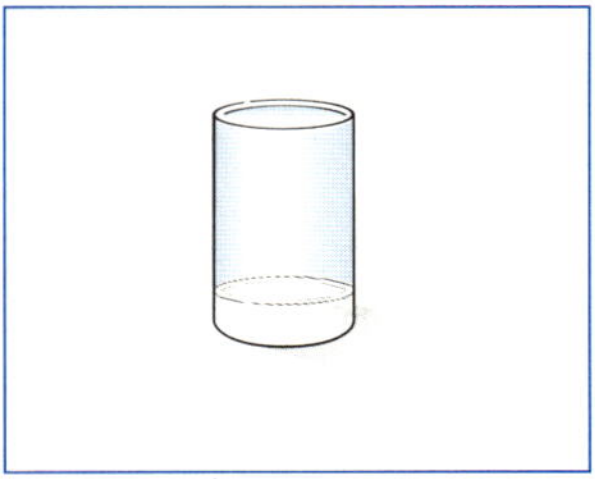

g) a .... milk

h) a .... milk

i) too .... people

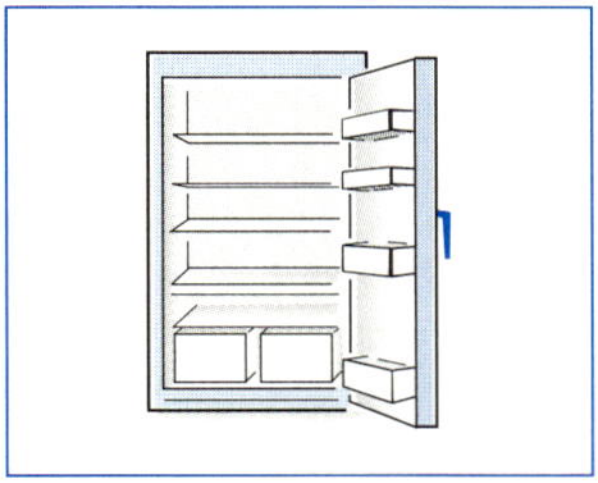

j) .... food

k) not .... money

l) .... inside

2. Vervollständigen Sie die Sätze mit den Ausdrücken aus dem Kasten.

much less all over least few little another most

a) I haven't got much money, but he's got even ....
b) You can only see the film if you're .... 18.
c) That cake was very nice. Could I have .... piece?
d) – I liked all of the paintings.
– Which one did you like ....?
e) He doesn't say .... He's quite shy.
f) Very .... people came because of the bad weather.
g) It leaves very .... money for our holiday.
h) He keeps .... his letters in a safe.
i) It's the .... I can do.

2001–4000

3. Unterstreichen Sie jeweils den richtigen Ausdruck.

a) There was a big *pile/mass/majority* of books on the floor.
b) She asked to see the *quantity/total/contents* of the box.
c) I rang four friends but *neither/none/only* of them answered.
d) – Have you got any books to read?
– Yes, *plenty of/several/a mass*.
e) *The majority students/The majority of students/The most students* live in flats.

2.3.2 *Grundzahlen*

1–2000

1. Schreiben Sie die Zahlen aus.

a) 13 ....
b) 4 ....
c) 6 ....
d) 80 ....
e) 40 ....
f) 21 ....
g) 5 ....
h) 17 ....

i) 15 . . . .
j) 53 . . . .
k) 44 . . . .
l) 36 . . . .
m) 100 . . . .
n) 12 . . . .
o) 1,000 . . . .
p) 11 . . . .
q) 9 . . . .

1–4000

2. Schreiben Sie die Ergebnisse aus.

a) Two multiplied by three is . . . .
b) Twelve divided by four is . . . .
c) If you subtract seven from eight, you get . . . .
d) Ten added to four is . . . .
e) A thousand multiplied by a million is a . . . .

Maße und Gewichte 2.3.3

1–4000

1. Vervollständigen Sie die Sätze.

a) There are 12 inches in a . . . .
b) There are 3 . . . . in a yard.
c) A . . . . is a few inches longer than a yard.
d) There are 453.59 . . . . in an English pound.
e) 2.2 pounds make a . . . .
f) A metric . . . . is 1,000 kg.
g) A kilometre is shorter than a . . . .
h) A litre is more than a . . . .
i) There are 100 . . . . in a metre.
j) This morning the doctor . . . . my height and . . . . me. I'm 1.65 . . . . tall and my . . . . is 49 kilograms.

Ordnung 2.4

Ordnungsbegriffe 2.4.1

1–4000

1. Welches Wort passt nicht? Streichen Sie es durch.

a) I bought my dad a new *set/group* of tools for Christmas.
b) Whose *row/turn* is it to do the washing-up?
c) Put all the surnames in alphabetical *row/order.*

d) This is very high-*class/quality* work.
e) He carefully *arranged/ordered* all the papers on the table.
f) This city is known for its high *degrees/levels* of smog in summer.
g) Rover and Ferrari are very different *brands/types* of cars.
h) He was thrown out of school for breaking the *rules/standards.*
i) What is your favourite television *row/series?*
j) It's the wrong *extent/size* – we need a much bigger kitchen.
k) I've just bought myself a *pair/pair of* digital bathroom scales.

2. Vervollständigen Sie die Sätze mit den Ausdrücken aus dem Kasten.

series	row	kind	
pair	degrees	class	order
size	brand	set	

a) It's much too big. Have you got a smaller . . . . ?
b) I don't like these cigarettes. Have you got another . . . .
c) I've only got one candlestick. I need a . . . .
d) There are only five teacups and saucers. It isn't a full . . . .
e) I don't like jazz. Have you got any other . . . . of music?
f) I always travel economy. I can't afford business . . . .
g) Our seats are K11 and K12. We must be in the . . . . behind you.
h) It's very cold outside. The temperature is only eight . . . . Celsius.
i) It wasn't just one mistake, it was a whole . . . . of errors.
j) You will come up onto the stage in . . . . of age: the youngest first, the oldest last.

Unterschied und Einteilung 2.4.2

1–2000

1. Vervollständigen Sie die Sätze mit den Ausdrücken aus dem Kasten.

else	others	same	another
regular	very much	very	special
only	not a	different	especially
rest	common	together	besides
part	single	alone	as ... as
like	than	piece	next

a) I've got a lot of those stamps. They're quite ....
b) – Have some more cake.
– Just a small ...., thanks.
c) She's the same size as her mother. She's .... tall .... her mother.
d) I'm still thirsty. Could I have .... glass of water?
e) We were expecting ten people and half of them didn't come – .... five turned up.
f) I can't see any difference. This picture looks the .... as the other.
g) A harpsichord is .... stringed instrument, it's a keyboard instrument.
h) We don't have wine every day, only on .... days like birthdays.
i) There's only a little mashed potato left – will you eat up the ....?
j) He doesn't look .... his brother at all.
k) I'm not .... I've got my next-door neighbour with me.
l) I like all kinds of cheese, ... Emmental.
m) The .... time you come, we must show you our holiday photographs.
n) – Would you like to come and stay with us?
– Yes, ...
o) These are sweet mandarins. The .... are a bit sour.
p) There's a .... service to London, with buses leaving every fifteen minutes.

q) You always see him .... with his twin brother.
r) What do you do .... watching television?
s) She's much cleverer .... you.
t) Is there anything .... we have to do?
u) – What's the new teacher like?
   – She's .... nice.
v) They're brother and sister, but they have completely .... personalities.
w) Which .... of the paper do you want?
x) I looked all over town, but I couldn't find a .... dress that I liked.

2001–4000

2. Welches Verb aus dem Kasten passt jeweils?

include | separate | combine | consist of | limit

a) ....: – business with pleasure; – history and geography; – both advantages

b) ....: – the egg whites from the yolks; – after ten years of marriage; – the boys from the girls

c) ....: – somebody's freedom; – the amount of sugar you eat; – a speech to ten minutes

d) ....: – drinks in the price; – someone in a conversation; – something in a list

e) ....: – several parts; – a beginning, a middle and an end; – milk, flour and butter

3. Welche Satzhälften aus der linken und rechten Spalte passen zusammen?

a) You can have either fish pie	p) to the rule.
b) Both my mother	q) but breakfast was extra.
c) I like to wear natural fibres,	r) between the two cars.
d) It's the exception	s) because they're not even similar.
e) The average family in Britain	t) and my grandfather were surgeons.
f) It isn't a very common bird,	u) except seafood.
g) I can't see any difference	v) which was much later than usual.
h) The price included accommodation,	w) in fact it's quite rare.
i) He eats anything	x) has 2.4 children.
j) They got back at four,	y) or roast beef.
k) You can't compare them	z) cotton and silk, for example.

a)	d)	g)	j) ....
b)	e)	h)	k) ....
c)	f)	i)	

4. Welches Wort passt jeweils? Unterstreichen Sie es.

a) What is the *opposite/contrary* of "sad"?
b) – Are you hungry?
– On the *opposite/contrary* – I had a three-course lunch, so I'm quite full.
c) Her behaviour hasn't been *normal/usual* lately.
d) Is that *typical/usual* of English people?
e) He has left all the doors open as *general/usual.*
f) I'm just an *average/ordinary* housewife.
g) The standard of his work is *average/middle.*
h) I want them to have a *general/whole* education.
i) The first course is fish and the *chief/main* course is chicken.

2.4.3 *Ordnungszahlen*

1–4000

1. Welche Kürzel fehlen nach diesen Ordnungszahlen? Schreiben Sie anschliessend die Zahlen vollständig aus.

a) 17.......... ....
b) 3.......... ....
c) 1.......... ....
d) 1,000.......... ....
e) 2.......... ....
f) 4.......... ....
g) 23.......... ....

2. Schreiben Sie die Ordnungszahlen in den folgenden Sätzen vollständig aus.

a) It's his 90th birthday next week. ....
b) The theatre's on 42nd street. ....
c) For the 100th time, don't touch it! ....
d) This is my 6th ice cream. ....
e) It's our 25th wedding anniversary today. ....
f) It was the 18th accident in a week. ....
g) He broke the record at the 33rd attempt. ....
h) I'm not celebrating my 21st birthday. ....

Ursache und Wirkung 2.5

1–4000

1. Vervollständigen Sie die Sätze mit den Ausdrücken aus dem Kasten.

condition due to relationship origin
as so because
reason result cause why
in order to therefore effect

a) She can't come .... of her father, who is very ill.
b) We were late, ... we crept in through the back door.
c) .... he's going away on business, I've decided to paint the house.
d) I can't see any .... why we shouldn't visit them.
e) What was the .... of his sudden death?
f) I've always had a good .... with my brothers and sisters.
g) He's deaf and .... can't attend a normal school.
h) I wonder what kind of .... his parents' divorce will have on him.
i) Air pollution is usually a .... of too many cars on the roads.
j) She lost her job .... back problems.
k) My mother said she would help me with my homework on .... that I help her with the housework.
l) .... catch the first flight, we had to get up at five o'clock in the morning.
m) I can't understand .... she isn't talking to me.
n) What's the .... of the word "vocabulary"?

2.6 Art und Weise

1–2000

1. Welcher Ausdruck aus dem Kasten passt jeweils?

at all	just	all
how	a bit	
also	almost	at least

a) ....: – did you do it?; I don't know – it happened; be careful – you hold that

b) ....: it's – too sweet for me; he's – strange, isn't he?; she's gone – too far

c) ....: I've – got a Ferrari; he likes chocolate, and – ice cream; we're – going to Spain

d) ....: that house is – right for two people; you're – the right height; we were – in time for the concert

e) ....: the children are – from Africa; we're – at home; my family are – musicians

f) ....: I've got – 800 stamps; – the room was warm; it'll be 10 o'clock –

g) ....: I – lost him at the airport; dinner is – ready; we're – there

h) ....: doesn't he go out –?; I don't like fish –; James isn't – well

2. Unterstreichen Sie jeweils den richtigen Ausdruck.

a) We've got a rottweiler *also/almost/too*.
b) *At least/Almost/Really* he said sorry.
c) I'd *mostly/hardly/rather* stay at home tonight.
d) *Besides/At least/Even*, it's a very expensive restaurant.
e) When do you *rather/usually/suddenly* see them?
f) – I like Schubert./*– I also/– I too/– I do too*.
g) I've *almost/really/hardly* had anything to eat.

3. Welche Ausdrücke passen? Haken Sie die Kästchen ab.

The children are
- ☐ usually
- ☐ really
- ☐ besides
- ☐ even
- ☐ all
- ☐ at all
- ☐ so
- ☐ mostly
- ☐ quite well-behaved.

4. *Hard* oder *hardly*? Unterstreichen Sie das richtige Wort.

a) My brother works *hard/hardly.*
b) My sister *hard/hardly* works at all.
c) You're *hard/hardly* trying.
d) I'm trying as *hard/hardly* as I can.
e) – Will he lend you the money?
– *Hard/Hardly.*

5. Ein einziges Wort fehlt. Welches ist es?

I'll learn English my . . . . , and you can learn it your . . . . By the . . . . , the quickest . . . . to learn a language is by practising every day – it's the hard . . . . , but it's the only . . . . that works.

ALLGEMEINES

2001–4000

6. Welche Ausdrücke passen jeweils? Haken Sie die Kästchen ab.

a) The house was
- ☐ partly
- ☐ largely
- ☐ merely
- ☐ scarcely
- ☐ nearly
- ☐ completely
- ☐ willingly finished.

b) We were
- ☐ partly
- ☐ absolutely
- ☐ merely
- ☐ generally
- ☐ nearly
- ☐ completely
- ☐ thoroughly delighted with the results.

c)
- ☐ Anyway,
- ☐ Somehow
- ☐ In any case,
- ☐ Instead,
- ☐ Though
- ☐ By chance
- ☐ Otherwise it worked out well.

2.7 Farben

1–4000

1. Welche Farbe assoziiert man am ehesten mit diesen Dingen?

a) grass, ecology, unripe fruit ....
b) death, coal, night ....
c) wedding, lily, snow ....
d) clouds, old person's hair, brain cells ....
e) baby girl, healthy cheeks, lipstick ....
f) suntan, beer, bread ....
g) sky, sea, aristocratic blood ....
h) sunset, blood, communism ....
i) canary, banana, telephone book ....

Formen

2.8

1–4000

1. Wie nennt man das?

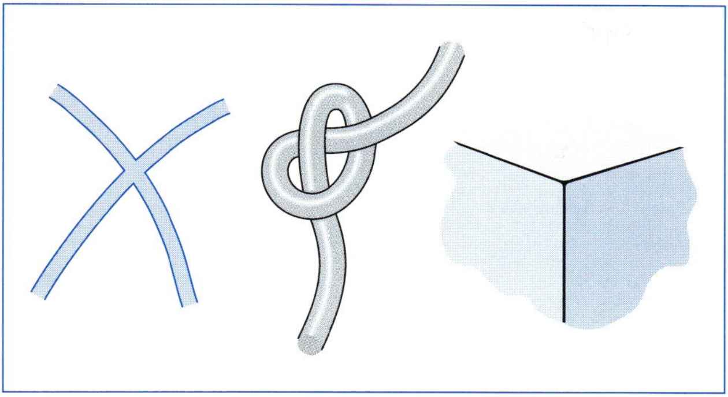

a) ....   b) ....   c) ....

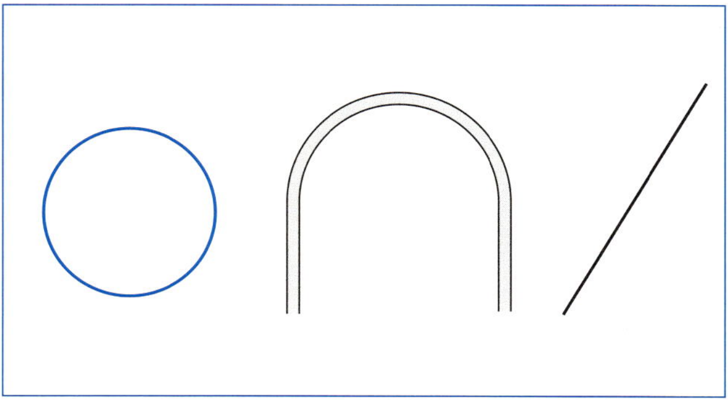

d) ....   e) ....   f) ....

2. Rund oder spitz? Tragen Sie die Gegenstände in die entsprechende Spalte ein.

	round	*pointed*
arrow	....	....
ball	....	....
tip	....	....
pin	....	....
earth	....	....
eye		
needle		
goldfish bowl		
balloon		
knife		

1–4000

1. Was geht hier vor? Vervollständigen Sie die Sätze.

a) The house is ....

b) The girl has .... the glass.

c) He's .... some tea.

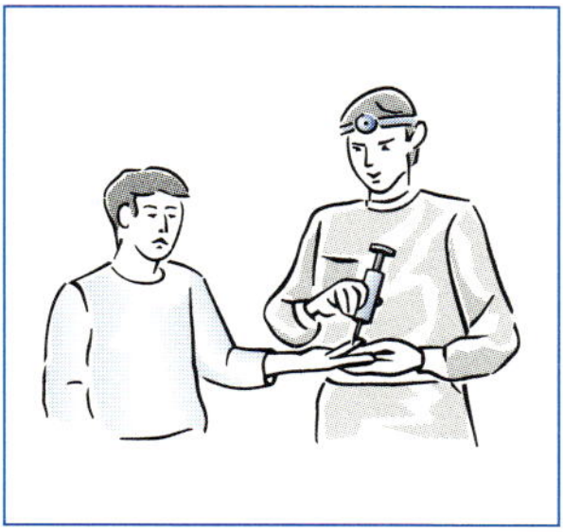

d) He's .... the boy's finger.

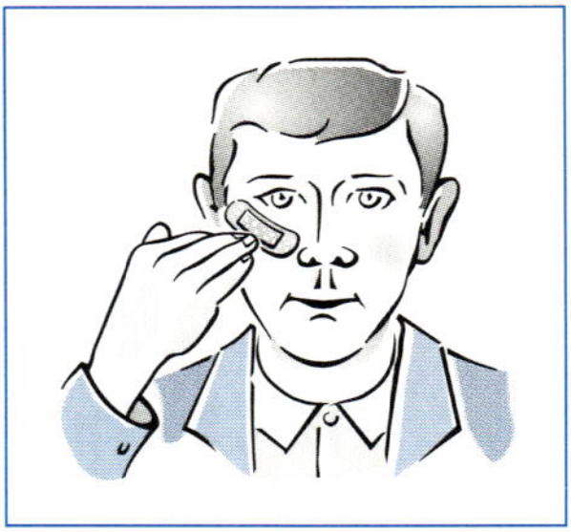

e) He has .... plaster on his face.

f) The sun is ....

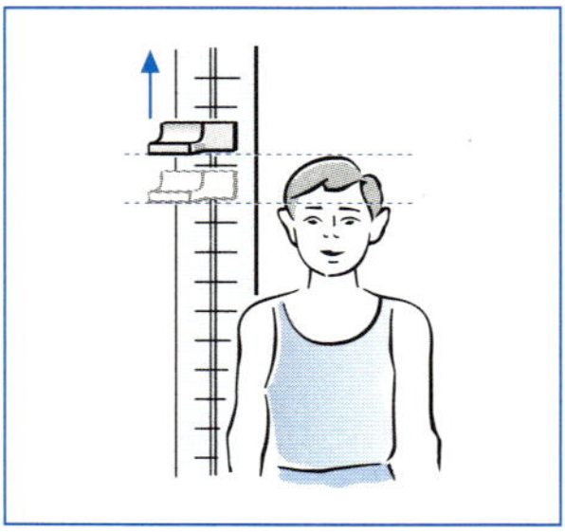

g) He's ....

h) She's.......... the doorbell.

i) The balloon is going to ....

j) He's .... his head.

2. Welches Verb aus dem Kasten fehlt jeweils? Setzen Sie es in die richtige Zeitform.

handle	treat	increase
introduce	spread	
strike	lean	spare
hit	belong	

a) – Who does this book .... to?
– It's mine.
b) I was crossing the road when I was .... by a bicycle.
c) He doesn't know how to .... problems.
d) I remember when seatbelts were first ....
e) This is an expensive watch – .... it with great care.
f) The aeroplane was .... by lightning, but nothing happened to us.
g) Mark was .... against the cupboard when suddenly it fell over.
h) Can you .... some milk? I haven't got any left.
i) .... the tablecloth on the grass and I'll put the food out.
j) They haven't .... our salary for four years, so I'm looking for a new job.

3. Womit reimt es sich? Unterstreichen Sie das richtige Wort.

a)	spread:	seed	bed
b)	beat:	meet	met
c)	break:	cake	peak
d)	bear:	hair	hear
e)	lower:	power	Goa
f)	pour:	shower	poor

3.2 Weitere Adjektive

1–2000

1. Fügen Sie das Gegenteil des unterstrichenen Wortes ein.

a) I don't like men with thick lips. I prefer .... lips.
b) This blanket is too heavy for the baby. Have you got a ....er one?
c) The biscuit tin was full this morning, and now it's completely ....
d) The door is supposed to be ...., not shut.
e) Don't keep switching the computer on and .... – it uses up too much electricity.
f) The US dollar is quite .... at the moment, but the Mexican Peso is getting weaker.
g) We live in a very large house, but now that the children have all moved out we're looking for a .... one.
h) She said the test would be easy, but it was quite ....
i) There's plenty of cold water, but there isn't any .... water for a bath.
j) Can you tell those noisy kids to be ....?
k) That coat looks so .... – haven't you got a more modern-looking one?

2. Welches Wort stimmt? Unterstreichen Sie es.

a) Have you seen the *last/latest* James Bond movie?
b) I have two *little/small* brothers and an older sister.
c) My grandfather was a *big/great* man. He was over two metres tall.
d) Do you have one or two *hot/warm* meals a day?
e) My parents have very *modern/new* ideas about bringing up children.
f) My sister eats too much junk food. That's why she's so *fat/thick.*

2001–4000

3. Welches Adjektiv aus dem Kasten passt am besten?

urgent	bright	bare	familiar
loose	huge	stiff	pure
steady	powerful	fresh	ancient

a) ....: hand, nerves, girlfriend, job
b) ....: day, sun, morning, star
c) ....: mountain, country, meal, car
d) ....: knot, screw, trousers, button
e) ....: gold, cotton, butter, luck
f) ....: face, voice, sound, view
g) ....: civilisation, world, times, history
h) ....: message, case, situation, need
i) ....: politician, engine, storm, personality
j) ....: leg, neck, collar, joints
k) ....: feet, hands, head, body
l) ....: fruit, milk, meat, fish

Strukturwörter 3.3

Pronomen und Artikel 3.3.1

1–4000

1. Welches Wort stimmt? Unterstreichen Sie es.

a) *Whom/Whose* pencil is this?
b) To *whom/who* are you writing?
c) *Who/Whom* is going with you?
d) There are three colours – *which/what* one would you like?
e) *This/These* papers can be thrown out.
f) Do you want this chair or *this/that* one over there?
g) There's plenty of food. Eat *whatever/whoever* you want.
h) *Whatever/Whoever* you bring home, they will be welcome in our house.
i) *What/Which* a lovely bunch of flowers!

2. Vervollständigen Sie die Lücken (z. B. *They're my best friends. I spend a lot of time with* <u>*them*</u>*.*).

a) Who is she? I don't know . . . .
b) Is that your father? I'd like to meet . . . .
c) What about . . . . ? I want to come too.
d) Don't worry about . . . ., we can manage on our own.
e) Who are those people? I don't recognize . . . .
f) You haven't got a serviette. Let me give . . . . this one.
g) – Is this your pen?
– Yes, it's . . . .
h) – Is that the Wilsons' car?
– Yes, I'm sure it's . . . .
i) I pricked . . . . while I was picking roses.
j) She's too small to look after . . . . She needs a babysitter.
k) Our neighbours drive the children to school and we look after their baby. That way we help . . . .
l) The light switches . . . . on automatically when you open the door.
m) That pigeon must have broken one of . . . . wings.
n) Come on children, help . . . . – there's plenty of food for everyone.
o) DIY is short for "do it . . . .".

3. Vervollständigen Sie die Sätze mit *some, any, something, anything, somebody* bzw. *anybody.*

a) – There's . . . . at the door.
– I can't see . . . .
b) – Have . . . . coffee.
– No thanks, I'm not allowed to have . . . . coffee.
c) I'm looking for . . . . nice to give to my Auntie Phyllis, but I can't find . . . . suitable.

4. Unterstreichen Sie jeweils den richtigen Ausdruck.

a) Does *every/everybody/each* want pudding?
b) I answered the phone but there was *anybody/not one/nobody* there.
c) *Whoever/Who/Which* it was will be punished.
d) He's *such a/so/so a* helpful boy.
e) *Anyone/No one/Whoever* knew him.

5. Übersetzen Sie.

a) Peter ist Schauspieler.

....

b) Der Hund hat sein Auge verletzt.

....

c) Es war so ein schöner Tag.

....

d) Sie hatte die Arme hinter dem Rücken.

....

e) Hast du ein besseres?

....

Hilfsverben 3.3.2

1–2000

1. Welches Verb stimmt? Unterstreichen Sie es.

a) You *mustn't/needn't* tell anyone. If you do, I'll beat you up.
b) – *Shall/Will* we go out for a drink?
   – That's a good idea.
c) – Am I allowed to ride on Steve's motorbike?
   – No, you *could/may* not ride on Steve's motorbike.
d) I *could/should* whistle when I was three.
e) Do you think you *could/would* help me with this shopping?
f) You don't *need/ought* to collect me from the disco.
g) I *ought/should* really go to the dentist.
h) – He never helps in the house.
   – Well, he *needs/ought* to.
i) They *could/would* rather go on holiday on their own.
j) Will he *can/be able to* walk after the operation?
k) Tell the children they *haven't to/mustn't* play with the stereo.
l) You *mustn't/needn't* come if you don't want to.
m) – Do you think she's at home?
   – She *might/must* be, but I'm not sure.
n) – Are they upstairs?
   – They *must/may* be because they're not downstairs and they haven't left the house.

3.3.3 *Weitere Präpositionen, Konjunktionen und Adverbien*

1–2000

1. Vervollständigen Sie die Sätze mit Hilfe der Wörter aus dem Kasten.

as (2x)	or	to (2x)	that
of	if	but	for
between	about (2x)	and	with
in	by	from	without

a) – Are you hungry .... thirsty?
– Both. I'm hungry .... thirsty.

b) On Sunday we walked .... Burford .... Cheltenham, and then had tea with friends who live in Cheltenham.

c) I knew you were talking .... me – my ears were burning.

d) .... you want to come, let us know.

e) He's so dependent on his mother, he doesn't go anywhere .... her.

f) You've never got any time .... me.

g) Do you want to pay .... cash or .... credit card?

h) It's just .... fast .... the other car.

i) He's hard-working .... he's a bit slow.

j) Are you absolutely sure .... you want to do it?

k) Which country is he president .... ?

l) Give him some food .... keep him quiet.

m) He has to travel a long distance .... his home and his office.

n) I always have water .... my whisky.

o) – How old is he?
– He must be .... forty now.

2001–4000

1. Welche Satzhälften aus der linken und rechten Spalte passen zusammen?

a) I'm happy to go	q) in spite of her age.
b) They gave her the job	r) such as Florida or Mexico.
c) You've sent me a cassette	s) although I warned them not to.
d) He won't get fit	t) whether he would like it.
e) I just don't know	u) for the sake of our friendship.
f) He was acting	v) instead of a CD.
g) You should go to a place with good weather,	w) unless he does some exercise.
h) Please do it	x) it happened last night.
i) They went up the mountain	y) as if he didn't know me.
j) According to Frank,	z) wherever you like.

a) .... d) .... g) .... i) ....
b) .... e) .... h) .... j) ....
c) .... f) ....

LÖSUNGEN

1.1 Der Mensch

1.1.1 *Körper und Wesen*

1.1.1.1 Körper

1. **a)** head **b)** face **c)** neck **d)** chest **e)** back **f)** heart **g)** stomach **h)** arm **i)** hand **j)** finger **k)** leg **l)** foot
2. **a)** hair **b)** nose **c)** eye **d)** ear **e)** mouth **f)** tooth **g)** tongue
3. **a)** forehead **b)** cheek **c)** lip **d)** shoulder **e)** elbow **f)** wrist **g)** thumb **h)** knee **i)** ankle **j)** toe
4. **a)** muscle **b)** brain **c)** sweat **d)** skin **e)** chin **f)** breath; breathe **g)** bone **h)** cheek **i)** breast **j)** waist **k)** fist **l)** nerve **m)** joint **n)** limb **o)** flesh **p)** heel

1.1.1.2 Aussehen

1. **a)** slim **b)** tall **c)** ugly **d)** big
2. d, b, c, a
3. **a)** handsome; good-looking **b)** pretty; attractive **c)** pretty; good-looking **d)** attractive; good-looking

1.1.1.3 Geist und Verstand

1. **a)** intelligent **b)** reasonable **c)** wise **d)** sensible **e)** skilful
2. **a)** remember **b)** thought **c)** understand **d)** thinking of **e)** realize
3. old and **wise;** has a good **memory;** she can **remember;** not **stupid** like me; a lot of other **skill**s; He isn't very **interested** in school; he has a lively **imagination;** she isn't very **keen** on boys; full of clever **idea**s; the classroom **fool;** drives Mrs Pinkerton **mad;** he pretends he can't **understand** her; to give you a first **impression;** fascinated by young **mind**s; we will all turn into **sensible** adults one day.

1.1.1.4 Charakter

1. **a)** serious – more serious – most serious
   b) cruel – crueller/more cruel – cruellest/most cruel
   c) honest – more honest – most honest
   d) careless – more careless – most careless
   e) polite – politer/more polite – politest/most polite
   f) fair – fairer – fairest

g) funny – funnier – funniest
h) generous – more generous – most generous
i) charming – more charming – most charming
j) lazy – lazier – laziest
k) proud – prouder – proudest
l) rude – ruder – rudest
m) shy – shyer – shyest

2. **a)** polite **b)** dishonest **c)** funny **d)** careless **e)** impatient **f)** bad **g)** unfair **h)** unfaithful

3. **a)** pride **b)** curious **c)** quality **d)** patience

4. **a)** coward **b)** courage **c)** polite **d)** generous **e)** friendly

Fühlen und Empfinden 1.1.1.5

1.

delighted	angry
glad	unhappy
happy	sad
excited	upset
	jealous
	disappointed

2. **a)** about **b)** with **c)** in **d)** of **e)** of **f)** at/by **g)** of **h)** for **i)** at/with

3. **a)** hate **b)** hope **c)** unhappy/sad **d)** unpleasant **e)** dissatisfied **f)** boring

4. **nervous** about meeting him; quite a **lonely** childhood; she **longed** for a boyfriend; a very **sensitive** young man who **liked/likes** quiet girls; two **pleasant** hours talking and laughing; great **fun** dancing.
Cathy was **surprised** but **delighted** to receive a phone call; he **felt** so **happy** after the last evening; he **hoped** they could meet again; Cathy shared these **feeling**s; she had **fallen** in love; the start of a very **exciting** romance

5. **a)** love **b)** fear **c)** shock **d)** sympathy **e)** pleasure

Gesundheit und Krankheit 1.1.1.6

1. **a)** temperature **b)** headache **c)** accident **d)** cold; flu **e)** health **f)** well **g)** sick **h)** pain **i)** hurt **j)** ill **k)** sick **l)** cough

2. **a)** He's **blind.** **b)** He's got **toothache.** **c)** She's got an **upset stomach.** **d)** She's got a **sore throat.** **e)** She's **deaf.** **f)** His finger is **bleeding.**

3. **a)** tremble **b)** fainted **c)** broke down **d)** recovered; heal **e)** injured **f)** swell

1.1.1.7 Leben und Tod

1. | *life* | *death* |
|---|---|
| birth | fatal |
| alive | funeral |
| survive | kill |
| exist | die |
| born | bury |
| grow up | dead body |

2. **a)** life **b)** death **c)** youth **d)** existence **e)** birth
3. birth, childhood, youth, old age, death
4. **a)** life **b)** live **c)** live **d)** alive; live; life
5. **a)** dead **b)** died **c)** Death **d)** died; death
6. **a)** Life is good. **b)** The life of the Eskimos is hard. / The Eskimos' life is hard. **c)** Death is hard/difficult to understand. **d)** The death of the three students was a shock.

1.1.2 *Aktivitäten*

1.1.2.1 Wachen und Schlafen

1. Jack: I'm **tired.** I think I'll go to **bed.**
   Roger: Do you need a lot of **sleep**?
   Jack: Only about ten hours a night.
   Roger: How long does it take you to **go** to sleep?
   Jack: A few seconds.
   Roger: And when you're **asleep** do you **dream**?
   Jack: Yes, I have very pleasant **dream**s – about sleeping.
   Roger: Hmm. What time do you usually **get** up in the mornings?
   Jack: As soon as I **wake up.**
   Roger: And when you're **awake** do you feel rested?
   Jack: Zzzzzzz…
   Roger: Oh dear, I think he's **fallen** asleep.

1.1.2.2 Sinneswahrnehmungen

1. **a)** look/see **b)** hear; listen **c)** touch; feel **d)** taste **e)** smell
2. senses
3. **see** Inspector Morse; I never **watch** TV. I prefer to **listen** to the radio. Did you **see/watch** the Oasis concert; a quiet evening **look**ing at my holiday photos. Could I **see** them; few months **watch**ing and **listen**ing to

Körperpflege 1.1.2.3

1.

g	f	**t**	a	d	h	i	e	f	s
s	**p**	**o**	**w**	**d**	**e**	**r**	**s**	b	o
c	d	**o**	i	r	e	t	**h**	t	u
x	i	**t**	u	d	n	**c**	**o**	**m**	**b**
k	c	**h**	a	o	n	l	**w**	**a**	r
b	k	**p**	s	**t**	**b**	x	**e**	**k**	w
i	**r**	**a**	**z**	**o**	**r**	r	**r**	**e**	t
t	t	**s**	t	**w**	**u**	l	o	**u**	l
b	**a**	**t**	**h**	**e**	**s**	**o**	**a**	**p**	q
u	w	**e**	q	**l**	**h**	s	a	m	g

Tätigkeiten 1.1.2.4

1. **a)** done **b)** making **c)** make **d)** done; made/done; done **e)** made; do **f)** make; do **g)** made; do

2. **a)** He goes to work from Monday to/till Thursday.
b) Do you like your new job?
c) That was a bad job/a bad piece of work.
d) Work starts at nine.

3. **a)** prepare **b)** work **c)** practise **d)** decide **e)** try **f)** act **g)** manage **h)** plan **i)** make **j)** do

4. a) b) c) e) h)

Umgang mit Dingen 1.1.2.5

1.

open	*cut*	*shake*	*catch*
door	finger	fist	fish
fridge	bread	finger	train
book	tree	medicine	ball
window	chin	tree	mouse
fist	head	head	
	hair	hair	

2. **a)** pressing **b)** tearing **c)** looking for **d)** painting **e)** changing **f)** knocking

3. **a)** unfold **b)** turn on **c)** find **d)** empty **e)** miss **f)** waste **g)** straighten **h)** open **i)** separate **j)** unwrap **k)** miss

4. **a)** held, held **b)** used, used **c)** burnt, burnt **d)** wound, wound **e)** pressed, pressed **f)** dug, dug **g)** found, found **h)** spoilt, spoilt **i)** sawed, sawn **j)** rubbed, rubbed **k)** hung, hung **l)** caught, caught **m)** lit, lit **n)** split, split **o)** shut, shut **p)** kept, kept **q)** tore, torn **r)** cut, cut

1.1.2.6 Bewegen von Gegenständen

1. **a)** push **b)** carry **c)** load **d)** raise **e)** send **f)** lay **g)** pick up **h)** lift **i)** pull **j)** put **k)** turn **l)** drag **m)** remove **n)** lower
2. **a)** Take the dog back to your friend.
   b) What have you brought into the house?
   c) Peter took him to his uncle.
   d) Could you bring me my tablets?

1.1.2.7 Geben und Nehmen

1. **a)** accept – annehmen **b)** keep – behalten **c)** split – teilen **d)** pass – reichen **e)** borrow – sich leihen **f)** lend – leihen **g)** get – bekommen **h)** give – geben **i)** share – sich teilen **j)** occupy – besetzen **k)** leave – lassen **l)** reserve – reservieren **m)** return – zurückbringen **n)** take – nehmen **o)** receive – erhalten
2. **borrow** the money from; David **lent** it; to **borrow** money; to **lend** me it

1.1.3 Lernen und Wissen

1. **a)** learn **b)** write **c)** know **d)** read
2. **a)** about/on **b)** in **c)** to **d)** on **e)** of **f)** by **g)** on **h)** to
3. **a)** invented **b)** created **c)** experience **d)** experiments **e)** ability **f)** volumes
4. **a)** library **b)** notebook **c)** poems **d)** novel **e)** type **f)** letters **g)** pages **h)** expert **i)** ink **j)** test **k)** writer **l)** volumes
5. **a)** studying **b)** learn **c)** study **d)** learnt **e)** learnt

Verhalten 1.1.4

Allgemeines Verhalten 1.1.4.1

1. a–z, b–u, c–v, d–y, e–w, f–x
2. hasn't got any **manners;** lots of bad **habits;** makes no **effort;** the **way** she treats me; in **charge** of the place; can't **stand** it; **miss** my parents; they used to **look after** me; the **memories** of a happy family life; my private **affairs**
3. a–w, b–x, c–u, d–v, e–z, f–y

Verhalten gegen Menschen 1.1.4.2

1. **a)** silent; disturb **b)** excuse; helped **c)** promise; power **d)** remind **e)** kind; help
2. **a) im**press **b) en**courage **c) con**fidence **d) for**give **e) in**sulted **f) in**fluence **g) per**suade **h) con**fused **i) re**presenting
3. **a)** fight **b)** curse **c)** lead **d)** convince **e)** fighting **f)** upset **g)** brag **h)** copy **i)** confidence
4. **a)** lies **b)** encourage **c)** excuse **d)** unkind **e)** noise
5. **a)** bet **b)** street **c)** ham **d)** pair **e)** shower **f)** find **g)** hide

Sprache und Sprechabsichten 1.1.5

Sprache 1.1.5.1

1. **a)** told; said **b)** speaking; told **c)** speak **d)** told **e)** said **f)** tell
2. **a)** whispering **b)** shouting **c)** crying **d)** discussion **e)** argument **f)** conversation
3. **a)** spelling **b)** expression **c)** pronunciation **d)** discussion **e)** speech
4. **a)** voice **b)** sentence **c)** word **d)** sound

Sprechabsichten 1.1.5.2

Auskunft 1.1.5.2.1

1. **a)** I have/I've got some advice/a piece of advice for you.
   b) The news is very interesting.
   c) What does this information mean?
2. **a)** ask; answer **b)** report; show **c)** give; send **d)** make **e)** give; send **f)** make **g)** explain **h)** explain; make **i)** give; send; explain **j)** show **k)** answer; send; report **l)** ask; recommend **m)** make; give; send **n)** give **o)** give; send

1.1.5.2.2 *Zustimmung und Ablehnung*

1. **a)** No, not. **b)** Yes well. **c)** I confess. **d)** Lie. **e)** I mean it's a good idea. **f)** Correct. **g)** In favour of.
2. **a)** Yes, **please. b)** No, **thanks. c)** Yes, **I am. d)** Yes, **we are. e)** Yes, **I/we do. f)** No, **he isn't. g)** No, **they don't.**
3. view; favour; agree; reply; correct; approve; object; admire; protest; praised; complain; argument; mind; refuse; agreement

1.1.5.2.3 *Gewissheit und Zweifel*

1. **Probably;** not absolutely **sure/certain;** no real **proof;** it would **seem possible,** indeed **probable;** I **certainly** haven't drunk; **perhaps** it was you; **impossible;** I **suppose** it was him; how can we be **sure/certain**
2.

certain	*uncertain*
reality	doubt
fact	hesitate
obvious	possibility
decision	maybe
prove	guess
actually	appear
clear	estimate

3. **a)** determined **b)** decided **c)** claims

1.1.5.2.4 *Wertung und Urteil*

1. **a)** easy – **easier – easiest**
   b) nice – **nicer – nicest**
   c) good – **better – best**
   d) bad – **worse – worst**
   e) difficult – **more difficult – most difficult**
   f) great – **greater – greatest**
2. **a)** bad **b)** ordinary **c)** boring **d)** worst **e)** difficult/complicated **f)** useless **g)** worthless **h)** unimportant **i)** badly
3. **a)** criticism **b)** fault **c)** satisfied **d)** perfect **e)** proves **f)** convenient **g)** suitable **h)** excellent
4. **a)** boring **b)** convenient **c)** terrible **d)** lovely **e)** precious **f)** suitable **g)** false **h)** slight
5. **a)** saying **b)** to mention **c)** to come **d)** in flying **e)** to see **f)** to be **g)** for coming **h)** by/in buying **i)** to get

Befehl und Verbot 1.1.5.2.5

1. **a)** I wasn't **allowed to go to the party.**
   b) He **made me stay at home and clean up.**
   c) Then **he ordered me to go to bed.**
   d) He **didn't/wouldn't allow me to read in bed.**
   e) I always **obey him.**
2. **a)** write **b)** not to swim **c)** from collapsing **d)** to paint **e)** read **f)** not to talk **g)** cut **h)** on buying

Wunsch und Bitte 1.1.5.2.6

1. **a)** I asked Jane help me. **b)** I suggest to eat at home. **c)** I wish I would be on holiday. **d)** She wants it be done today. **e)** What was his last demand before he died? **f)** Our will is to reach Phoenix tonight.

Begrüßung und Abschied 1.1.5.2.7

1. Good morning! Good afternoon! Good evening! Good night!
2. **a)** Mrs Humphrey **b)** Ms Stevens/Miss Stevens **c)** Ms Smith **d)** Mr Bartlett **e)** Mr Johnson

Häufige Redewendungen 1.1.5.3

1. a–s, b–z, c–v, d–x, e–q, f–w, g–u, h–r, i–y, j–p, k–t
2. **a)** Help yourself! **b)** How much are the/these apples? **c)** Would you like some tea/a cup of tea? **d)** Would you please stand up? **e)** Thank you (very much)./Thanks (very much)./ Thanks a lot. **f)** Sorry!/I'm sorry!/Excuse me! **g)** Sorry?/Pardon? **h)** How are you? **i)** What's the matter?
3. **a)** Have fun! **b)** – I'm tired. – Me too./So am I. **c)** – I like him. – Me too./So do I. **d)** Oh dear! **e)** Leave us alone! **f)** Get out! **g)** Beat it!/Get lost! **h)** Here you are! **i)** – I'm not tired. – Nor/ Neither am I. **j)** – I don't like it. – Nor/Neither do I.

Der Mensch und die Gesellschaft 1.1.6

Identifizierung 1.1.6.1

1. **a)** baby **b)** children **c)** girl **d)** boy **e)** woman **f)** man **g)** lady **h)** gentleman
2. **a)** gentlemen **b)** ladies **c)** children **d)** babies **e)** women **f)** people
3. **What's** your name; that's a nice **name;** what's your **surname/family name;** What do you **call** your dog; So it's **called;** That's a big **name;** What **sex** is it; he's got to be **male**

1.1.6.2 Familie

1. **a)** grandparents **b)** brother **c)** sister-in-law **d)** daughter **e)** sons **f)** cousins **g)** uncles **h)** sister; aunt **i)** mother; father **j)** brother; grandfather **k)** husband **l)** parents-in-law **m)** uncle; widow **n)** nephews; niece **o)** grandchildren **p)** granddaughters; grandsons **q)** wife **r)** parents
2. most of them **relative**s of the happy **couple**; The **bride** wore; the **groom** was in; young, **single** people; also **married** couples; the **bride**'s father; had just got **engaged**; **heir**s to a large fortune

1.1.6.3 Soziale Bindungen

1. **a)** girlfriend **b)** enemies **c)** partners **d)** public **e)** common
2. **a)** public **b)** company **c)** society **d)** people **e)** colleague **f)** member **g)** strangers **h)** community

1.1.6.4 Berufe

1. **a)** typist **b)** cook **c)** mechanic **d)** farmer **e)** photographer **f)** electrician **g)** housewife **h)** pharmacist/chemist
2. **a)** My sister is a secretary. **b)** My brother-in-law is a businessman. **c)** I want to be an engineer. **d)** My uncles are all butchers or tailors. **e)** I'm a trainee.
3. **a)** businesswoman **b)** sales representative **c)** professional **d)** trainee; apprentice

1.1.6.5 Soziale Situation

1. a–z, b–u, c–y, d–x, e–s, f–w, g–t, h–v

1.1.6.6 Soziales Verhalten

1. **a)** It is a custom here to give guests the biggest bed.
   b) How many families live in this neighbourhood?
   c) When are you going to visit your grandparents?
   d) I have a present for you.
   e) Congratulations on passing your test!
   f) He says he has invited fifty people to his party.
   g) Do you have many social problems in this area?

2. **a)** Let me show you where your room is.
   b) Are you coming to the party?
   c) Can we meet again some time?
   d) I've got a date with a colleague from work this evening.
   e) I think you should go and see a doctor.

3. **a)** celebrate **b)** waved **c)** invitation **d)** joining **e)** introduce
   f) getting along **g)** wedding **h)** visitors **i)** contact

4. **a)** I'm getting married **to** my boyfriend next summer.
   b) Welcome **to** London!
   c) May I introduce you **to** my father?
   d) **She** is a very good hostess./He is a very good **host.**
   e) Only twenty people took part **in** the competition.
   f) The crowds waved **to/at us.**
   g) After ten years of marriage, they are now **separated.**

Schicksal und Zufall 1.1.7

1. what **happened;** there was a **fire;** very **dangerous;** real **trouble** because we **lost** our way; we were very **lucky;** he **succeeded** in finding us; to **safety;** amazing **luck;** he **saved** our lives; you're **famous; lucky** to be alive

2. **a)** bad luck **b)** failure **c)** safety **d)** dangerous **e)** create
   f) destruction **g)** unfortunately **h)** win

3. **a)** mystery **b)** opportunity **c)** emergency **d)** difficulty
   e) situation **f)** rescue **g)** explode **h)** destroy **i)** occasion
   j) adventure **k)** fortunately **l)** condition **m)** advantage

4. **a)** mystery **b)** advantage **c)** emergency **d)** event

5. **a)** of **b)** by **c)** on **d)** in **e)** for **f)** to **g)** for **h)** to

Alltagswelt 1.2

Der Mensch und sein Zuhause 1.2.1

Haus und Wohnung 1.2.1.1

1. **a)** garden **b)** gate **c)** door **d)** window **e)** roof **f)** wall
   g) stairs **h)** toilet **i)** bathroom **j)** bedroom **k)** living room
   l) kitchen

2. **a)** **first** floor
   second floor
   third floor
   b) They've moved into a new **apartment.**
   c) Let's take the **elevator.**
   d) Where's the **bathroom/restroom?**

3. on three **storeys;** down in the **basement;** a large **dining room;** a lovely stucco **ceiling;** beautifully **furnished; Upstairs** there are three bedrooms. The **front** of the house; attractive **chimneys;** a few **cracks;** needs a little **paint;** we've got to **move**

1.2.1.1 Einrichtung

1. **a)** chair **b)** bed **c)** cupboard **d)** table **e)** desk **f)** bench **g)** furniture

2. **a)** wardrobe **b)** curtain **c)** lamp **d)** stove

3. **a)** fridge **b)** freezer **c)** oven **d)** wardrobe **e)** pillow **f)** blanket **g)** armchair **h)** sofa **i)** carpet **j)** drawer **k)** cushion

1.2.1.3 Gegenstände und Geräte

1. **a)** ladder **b)** handbag **c)** scissors **d)** umbrella **e)** candle **f)** basket **g)** pencil **h)** screwdriver **i)** bucket **j)** wallet **k)** ballpoint **l)** handkerchief

2. light bulb *(Glühbirne),* scales *(Waage),* saw *(Säge),* ladder *(Leiter),* clock *(Uhr),* wastepaper basket *(Papierkorb),* box of screws *(Schachtel Schrauben),* rope *(Seil),* hose *(Schlauch)*

3. **a)** Where are my glasses?
b) I need a mirror and some/a pair of scissors.
c) These scales are digital.

4. **a)** thread, string, rope **b)** needle, scissors, saw **c)** wallet, handbag, basket **d)** needle, nail, key **e)** match, lighter, ashtray

1.2.1.4 Sauberkeit

1. so **dirty;** is a **mess** too; have it all **clean** and **tidy;** in the **dishwasher;** do the **laundry** – fill the **washing machine** up; those **stain**s on the tablecloth; after you've **dusted** the furniture you can **polish** the dining-room table; **wipe** all the kitchen surfaces; a new **broom** in the cupboard; use it to **sweep** the steps; don't forget to **wash** your hands

1.2.2 *Kleidung und Schmuck*

1. **a)** ring **b)** glove **c)** trousers **d)** hat **e)** shoes **f)** watch **g)** jacket **h)** suit **i)** skirt **j)** coat **k)** shirt **l)** pocket **m)** buttons **n)** dress

2. **a)** collar **b)** belt **c)** zip **d)** boots **e)** heel **f)** jewellery **g)** pearls **h)** scarf **i)** sleeve **j)** diamonds **k)** blouse **l)** tights

3. **a)** fit **b)** try on **c)** put on **d)** sews; knitted **e)** take off **f)** change **g)** wear

Arbeitswelt 1.2.3

Fabrik und Werkstatt 1.2.3.1

1. **a)** Could you repair my car today?
b) We'll have to get some spare parts.
c) The service is very quick and friendly/friendly and quick.
d) He has a workshop with lots of tool.
e) The industrial nations are the richest./The richest are the industrial nations.
f) It took him ten minutes to fix the window.
g) My brother works in the furniture factory down the road.
h) When are they going to mend the toilet?

Wirtschaftsleben 1.2.3.2

Allgemeines 1.2.3.2.1

1. **a)** unemployed **b)** busy **c)** wages **d)** sale **e)** order **f)** offered **g)** pay **h)** firm **i)** business **j)** goods

2. **a)** product, production **b)** manager, management **c)** competitor, competition **d)** employer, employee, employment

3. **a)** economic **b)** bargain **c)** imports **d)** Trade **e)** property **f)** Demand **g)** employment **h)** produced **i)** manager

Geschäft 1.2.3.2.2

1. **a)** supermarket (*Supermarkt*) **b)** shopping (*Einkaufen*) **c)** drugstore (*Drogerie*) **d)** advertising (*Werbung*) **e)** department (*Abteilung*)

2. **a)** bought **b)** sold **c)** dealt in

Geld 1.2.4

1. **a)** cash **b)** price **c)** spends **d)** saving **e)** spent

2. **a)** in/to **b)** for/on **c)** of **d)** in **e)** for **f)** in

3. **a)** expensive **b)** spend **c)** buy **d)** save **e)** cash

4. **a)** coins **b)** loan **c)** interest **d)** owe **e)** currency **f)** afford **g)** charge **h)** profit **i)** income **j)** hire **k)** insurance **l)** value

5. **a)** in **b)** on **c)** per; per **d)** to **e)** of **f)** on **g)** on

1.2.5 *Ämter und Behörden*

1. a–x, b–z, c–y, d–v, e–u, f–w

1.2.6 *Post- und Fernmeldewesen*

1.2.6.1 Post

1. **a)** letter **b)** envelope **c)** address **d)** stamp **e)** postcard **f)** parcel

2. I write the **letter;** put it in an **envelope**, write the **address**; and the **sender**'s **address** on the back; put a **stamp** and an **airmail** sticker on it; the nearest **letterbox** to **post** it; the **postage** for Canada; to the **post office**

1.2.6.2 Telefon

1. **a)** hang up *(auflegen)* **b)** phonecard *(Telefonkarte)* **c)** telephone *(Telefon; anrufen)* **d)** local call *(Ortsgespräch)* **e)** phone box *(Telefonzelle)*

2. **a)** phonecard **b)** operator **c)** long-distance **d)** engaged **e)** fax **f)** answer **g)** dial

1.2.7 *Rechtswesen*

1.2.7.1 Rechtsprechung

1. **a)** arrested **b)** court **c)** confessed **d)** judge **e)** law

2. **a)** punishment **b)** accused of **c)** prisoners **d)** jail **e)** verdict

3. **a)** are **b)** don't **c)** they don't **d)** he knows

1.2.7.2 Strafbares Verhalten

1. **a)** rob **b)** shoot **c)** steal **d)** swindle **e)** kill **f)** force

2.

person	*crime*	*verb*
robber	murder	steal
thief	robbery	kill
burglar	violence	murder
criminal	offence	shoot

3. **a)** shot **b)** stole **c)** wrong **d)** illegal **e)** murder **f)** violent **g)** forced **h)** robbery **i)** suspect **j)** guilty

Arzt und Krankenhaus 1.2.8

1. 3,4,6,1,7,5,2,8
2. **a)** dentist **b)** operation **c)** specialist **d)** surgeon **e)** waiting room **f)** medicine **g)** patients **h)** poison

Schule und Universität 1.2.9

1. **a)** teach **b)** study **c)** learn **d)** translate
2. **a)** student **b)** pupils **c)** teacher
3. **a)** mathematics/maths **b)** physics **c)** geography **d)** history **e)** chemistry **f)** biology
4.

g	f	**s**	**d**	**s**	**c**	**h**	**o**	**o**	**l**
x	g	**t**	**i**	d	e	l	s	g	o
e	**d**	**u**	**c**	**a**	**t**	**i**	**o**	**n**	d
x	i	**d**	**t**	d	n	r	o	**t**	b
a	c	**y**	**i**	o	**r**	p	w	**e**	r
m	k	**h**	**o**	**m**	**e**	**w**	**o**	**r**	**k**
i	r	a	**n**	o	**p**	s	r	**m**	t
t	t	s	**a**	**t**	**o**	**p**	**i**	**c**	l
b	a	t	**r**	e	**r**	k	a	o	q
u	w	e	**y**	l	**t**	**e**	**a**	**c**	**h**

5. **a)** failed **b)** pass **c)** taken **d)** passed

Interessen 1.3

Kunst 1.3.1

Bildende Kunst 1.3.1.1

1. **a)** paint; sculptor **b)** museum; exhibition **c)** style; artist **d)** pictures; gallery **e)** drawing; print **f)** paintings; art **g)** painter; sculptures
2. **a)** drew **b)** sculptor **c)** artist **d)** prints

Theater, Film und Fernsehen 1.3.1.2

1. **a)** actor **b)** plays **c)** ticket **d)** stage **e)** audience **f)** scenes **g)** acts **h)** comedy **i)** cinema **j)** screen
2. **a)** perform **b)** scenes **c)** performances **d)** role **e)** movies **f)** comedy **g)** play **h)** directed

1.3.1.3 Musik

1\.

instruments	*professions*	*groups of musicians*
violin	conductor	orchestra
guitar	composer	choir
piano	musician	band

2\. **a)** music **b)** tune **c)** rhythm **d)** concert **e)** strings **f)** instrument **g)** musical **h)** sing; play **i)** singer; songs

1.3.2 *Kommunikationsmittel*

1\. **a)** broadcast **b)** publish **c)** interview **d)** channel **e)** programme **f)** headline **g)** television **h)** newspaper **i)** magazine

2\. **a)** press **b)** radio **c)** media

3\. **a)** issue **b)** channel **c)** live **d)** published **e)** announced

1.3.3 *Erholung und Freizeit*

1.3.3.1 Erholung

1\. **a)** on **b)** for **c)** take **d)** have **e)** for

1.3.3.2 Freizeitbeschäftigungen und Hobbies

1\. **a)** photograph **b)** dancing **c)** slide **d)** climbing **e)** playing **f)** hunting

2\. **a)** Michael won a **prize** for his essay on African elephants.
b) That's a lovely **photograph** of your grandparents.
c) I think the last piece of this **jigsaw puzzle** is missing.
d) I see you've got a new stereo set. Those **speakers** are very big!
e) They've gone **hiking** in the mountains.

3\.

photography	*home entertainment*
slide	stereo
print	tape
camera	speaker
photograph	cassette recorder
colour film	TV

1.3.3.3 Vergnügen und Genuss

1\. **a)** joke **b)** pleased **c)** enjoy **d)** cigarettes; tobacco **e)** cigars; pipe **f)** smoker **g)** enjoy; entertaining **h)** entertainment

Sport 1.3.4

1. **a)** diving **b)** skiing **c)** swimming **d)** sailing **e)** running **f)** rowing **g)** riding **h)** kicking

2.

o	q	s	d	f	**t**	k	j	**s**	g
r	**e**	**f**	**e**	**r**	**e**	**e**	e	**p**	s
a	p	**o**	w	d	**a**	m	s	**e**	o
c	**g**	**o**	**a**	**l**	**m**	**a**	**t**	**c**	**h**
k	i	**t**	d	y	e	r	o	**t**	n
e	c	**b**	s	x	r	l	**s**	**a**	l
t	**r**	**a**	**i**	**n**	b	i	**c**	**t**	w
f	h	**l**	l	w	r	**p**	**o**	**o**	**l**
b	**a**	**l**	**l**	d	h	l	**r**	**r**	l
g	**a**	**t**	**h**	**l**	**e**	**t**	**e**	u	n

3. **a)** competition **b)** finals **c)** stadium **d)** race **e)** champion; coach **f)** medal **g)** whistle **h)** score

Öffentliches Leben 1.4

Staatswesen 1.4.1

Staat und Politik 1.4.1.1

1. **a)** border **b)** home **c)** foreigner **d)** countries **e)** minister **f)** queen **g)** president **h)** prince **i)** politics **j)** party

2. **a)** politician **b)** flag **c)** elect **d)** crisis

3. **a)** divide **b)** dependent **c)** emigration **d)** international **e)** opponent **f)** minority

4. **a)** state (United States) **b)** speech **c)** spy **d)** security (Security Council) **e)** republic (Irish Republic) **f)** Parliament **g)** democracy

Krieg und Frieden 1.4.1.2

1. **a)** peace **b)** defended **c)** disarmed **d)** civilians **e)** enemy **f)** victory

2.

troops	*weapons*	*verbs*
navy	bomb	attack
officer	arms	march
general	sword	occupy
army	gun	fight

3. **a)** arms/army **b)** flight **c)** resistance **d)** defence **e)** attack **f)** occupation **g)** fight/battle

1.4.2 *Kirche und Religion*

1. **a)** church **b)** bells **c)** angel **d)** devil **e)** monk **f)** nun

2. **a)** god **b)** pray **c)** Christmas **d)** service **e)** believe **f)** religion **g)** kneel **h)** sin **i)** faith **j)** Easter

3. **a)** The priest/minister says (that) good people go to heaven.
b) Do you believe in hell?
c) She's a Christian.
d) We celebrate Christ's birth/the birth of Christ at Christmas.

1.5 Umwelt

1.5.1 *Dorf und Stadt*

1. **a)** village **b)** city **c)** city centre **d)** square **e)** farm **f)** tower **g)** fence

2. **a)** road **b)** street **c)** road **d)** road **e)** street

3. **a)** fountain **b)** zoo **c)** monument **d)** cathedral **e)** ruins **f)** cemetery **g)** hut **h)** grave

4. **a)** area **b)** surroundings **c)** suburbs **d)** population **e)** local **f)** capital

1.5.2 *Landschaft*

1. **a)** forest **b)** valley **c)** coast **d)** field **e)** river **f)** park **g)** lake **h)** mountains **i)** beach **j)** path

2. **a)** river **b)** mountain **c)** forest **d)** beach **e)** lake **f)** view **g)** ground

3. **a)** dry **b)** green **c)** steep **d)** hard **e)** deep **f)** rich **g)** flat **h)** strong **i)** tropical

4. **a)** slope **b)** cave **c)** canals **d)** bay **e)** sand

1.5.3 *Natur*

1.5.3.1 Allgemeines

1. **a)** steam **b)** cool **c)** light **d)** gas **e)** shade

2. **a)** shadow **b)** shade **c)** shade **d)** shadow

Tierwelt 1.5.3.2

1. **a)** butterfly **b)** whale **c)** snake **d)** bull **e)** bee **f)** cock **g)** goat **h)** spider **i)** donkey **j)** monkey **k)** elephant **l)** fox

2.

birds	*insects*	*four-legged creatures*
turkey	spider	lion
chicken	wasp	rabbit
duck	mosquito	deer
pigeon	beetle	pig

3. **a)** geese **b)** calves **c)** mice **d)** fish **e)** sheep **f)** wolves **g)** deer

4. **a)** bee **b)** snake **c)** dog **d)** shark **e)** fox **f)** rabbit **g)** whale **h)** shark **i)** pig **j)** whale

5.

a) sting	**stung**	**stung**	*stechen*
b) bite	**bit**	**bitten**	*beißen*
c) fly	**flew**	**flown**	*fliegen*
d) feed	**fed**	**fed**	*füttern*
e) breed	**bred**	**bred**	*züchten*

Pflanzenwelt 1.5.3.3

1. **a)** tree **b)** branch **c)** trunk **d)** root **e)** leaf **f)** mushroom

2. grow **flower**s; some lovely rose **bush**es. He **grow**s almost everything from **seed**s; ready to **plant**; a few **fruit** trees; when they're in **blossom;** cutting the **grass;** trimming the **hedge;** pulling out **weed**s

3. **a)** grain **b)** grass **c)** maize **d)** grow **e)** bushes **f)** crops **g)** harvest

Himmel und Erde 1.5.3.4

1. **a)** north **b)** northeast **c)** east **d)** southeast **e)** south **f)** southwest **g)** west **h)** northwest

2. **a)** sun **b)** moon **c)** star **d)** earth

3. **a)** earth **b)** sky **c)** map **d)** lake **e)** Sea

4. **a)** The moon rose at six o'clock.
   b) The sun has gone down already.
   c) The sun hasn't shone for five days now.
   d) The astronaut was in space for four months.
   e) The sky is grey.

5. **a)** tide **b)** sunset **c)** rays **d)** The north. **e)** universe

1.5.4 *Wetter und Klima*

1. **a)** weather **b)** rainy **c)** frost **d)** storm **e)** temperatures **f)** lightning **g)** sunshine **h)** climate
2. **a)** clouds **b)** thunderstorm **c)** rain **d)** fog **e)** lightning **f)** frost **g)** snow **h)** blow **i)** freezes **j)** mist

1.5.4 *Umweltprobleme*

1. **a)** environment **b)** unleaded **c)** smog **d)** waste **e)** recycle **f)** pollution **g)** dump **h)** acid **i)** catalytic converter

1.6 Technik und Materialien

1.6.1 *Energie und Technik*

1. **a)** machine **b)** engine **c)** pump **d)** pipe **e)** electricity **f)** power **g)** spring
2. **a)** mechanical **b)** solar **c)** technical; technological **d)** electric; electrical **e)** electronic **f)** nuclear
3. **a)** cable **b)** tube **c)** electricity **d)** engineering **e)** solar **f)** switch

1.6.2 *Informationstechnik*

1. **a)** hardware **b)** software **c)** data **d)** keyboard **e)** file **f)** hard disk **g)** floppy disk **h)** PC **i)** word processing **j)** printer

1.6.3 *Materialien*

1. **a)** cotton **b)** stone **c)** wool **d)** soft **e)** wooden **f)** metal
2.

v	**p**	**l**	**a**	**s**	**t**	**i**	**c**	z	w
r	e	f	e	r	**i**	**r**	**o**	**n**	g
h	g	t	f	**c**	**n**	e	**p**	w	c
s	**t**	**e**	**e**	**l**	v	r	**p**	n	j
i	a	s	x	**o**	y	p	**e**	f	d
l	**l**	**e**	**a**	**t**	**h**	**e**	**r**	e	c
k	s	i	t	**h**	k	h	k	**l**	e
d	t	b	c	**r**	**u**	**b**	**b**	**e**	**r**
t	r	u	s	f	s	q	z	**a**	c
a	k	m	r	d	s	s	w	**d**	r

3. **a)** brick **b)** artificial **c)** solid **d)** chemicals **e)** an artificial **f)** fuel

Essen und Trinken 1.7

Allgemeines 1.7.1

1. very **hungry;** toast for **breakfast**; any **lunch;** he has a big **snack:** he **eat**s two bags of crisps; he **swallow**s everything so fast, without **chew**ing it properly; he is so **thirsty** that he has to **drink** about four glasses; time for **dinner;** the main **dish;** room for **dessert;** during the whole **meal;** junk **food;** an **appetite** like a horse

Lebensmittel 1.7.2

Allgemeines 1.7.2.1

1. jam, cheese, egg, salad, honey, butter

2.

sweet	*not sweet*
sugar	chips
sweets	pepper
chocolate	milk
ice cream	bread
cake	egg
jam	potato

3. **a)** salad **b)** soup **c)** fat **d)** chocolate **e)** egg

4. **a)** We need a loaf of bread.
b) I like jam, but not marmalade.
c) Do you like (potato) crisps?
Do you like (potato) chips?
d) Chips are full of fat.
French fries are full of fat.
e) I've only got a tin of soup.
I've only got a can of soup.

Fleisch und Fisch 1.7.2.2

1. **a)** chicken **b)** pork **c)** beef **d)** veal

2. **a)** bacon **b)** sausage **c)** steak **d)** chop

3. **a)** meat **b)** lean **c)** tough **d)** raw **e)** tender **f)** ham; bacon; pork *oder* bacon; ham; pork **g)** veal **h)** seafood

Obst und Gemüse 1.7.2.3

1. **a)** cherries **b)** nuts **c)** plum **d)** peas **e)** grapes **f)** pear **g)** banana **h)** carrot **i)** onion **j)** apple **k)** lemon **l)** beans **m)** lettuce **n)** strawberry **o)** cabbage

2.

fruit	*vegetables*
plum	tomato
pear	cabbage
strawberry	bean
cherry	pea
orange	onion
grapes	carrot

3. *fresh salad:* onion, herbs, carrot, lettuce, lemon
fruit salad: grapes, apple, banana, cherries, lemon

1.7.2.4 Getränke

1. **a)** juice **b)** soft drink **c)** barrel **d)** tea

2. **a)** coffee **b)** wine **c)** barrel **d)** drunk **e)** sweet **f)** soft **g)** tea **h)** alcohol **i)** refreshments

1.7.3 *Zubereitung der Speisen*

1. **a)** spread **b)** boil, stir **c)** fry, boil **d)** fry, boil, roast **e)** boil, stir **f)** fry, boil **g)** fry, bake, boil, roast **h)** fry, spread **i)** bake **j)** boil, spread

2.

slice	*drop*
bread	milk
cake	wine
tomato	lemon
lemon	beer
beef	soup
cheese	alcohol

1.7.4 *Geschirr und Besteck*

1. **a)** plate **b)** glass **c)** knife **d)** fork **e)** spoon **f)** cup

2. **a)** saucer **b)** bowl **c)** pan **d)** fork **e)** tablecloth; china **f)** kettle **g)** lid **h)** plate **i)** set **j)** tray **k)** handle **l)** opener **m)** cork

1.7.5 *Restaurant*

1. **a)** waitress **b)** set lunch **c)** pub **d)** bar **e)** self-service **f)** order **g)** tips **h)** service

Reise und Verkehr 1.8

Reise 1.8.1

1. **a)** catch **b)** way **c)** run **d)** guide **e)** stay **f)** timetable **g)** abroad **h)** customs; luggage **i)** hotel **j)** passenger **k)** travel **l)** leave
2. **a)** arrival **b)** miss **c)** leave
3. **a)** went **b)** stayed **c)** caught **d)** missed **e)** ran **f)** left
4. **a)** tourist **b)** accommodation **c)** luggage
5. **a)** check in, pick up, pack **b)** declare, pick up, pack **c)** check in, land
6. **a)** travel **b)** checked in **c)** camping **d)** started **e)** sightseeing

Verkehr 1.8.2

Straßenverkehr 1.8.2.1

Allgemein 1.8.2.1.1

1. **a)** road, path, river, bridge **b)** motorcycle, bicycle **c)** car, bus
2. **a)** pedestrian **b)** motorway **c)** crossroads **d)** driver **e)** park **f)** petrol **g)** bend **h)** traffic **i)** garage
3. **a)** belt **b)** limit **c)** rush **d)** driving **e)** petrol **f)** lights **g)** helmet **h)** park **i)** stop
4. **a)** freeway/expressway **b)** driver's license **c)** gas **d)** parking lot **e)** gas station

Fahrzeuge 1.8.2.1.2

1. **a)** bicycle **b)** lorry **c)** car **d)** caravan **e)** motorcycle **f)** bus **g)** truck **h)** tram **i)** taxi
2. **a)** motorcycle **b)** taxi **c)** trailer **d)** bike **e)** vehicle **f)** coach **g)** wheels **h)** caravan

Eisenbahn 1.8.2.2

1. by **underground;** I love **rail** travel; I took the **train** to see my cousin; After queuing at the ticket **office;** time to sit in the **waiting** room; slowly wandering to **platform** 6. I was looking for **carriage** number 121; big, light **compartment;** as soon as it moved out of the **station** I went to the dining **car;** I had to **change** at Newton Abbot; catch my **connection;** I asked the **guard;** I enjoy travelling by **train**

1.8.2.3 Flugzeug

1. **a)** flights **b)** airport **c)** wings **d)** jets **e)** take off **f)** takeoff

1.8.2.4 Schiff

1. **a)** ship **b)** boat **c)** captain **d)** sailor **e)** crossing **f)** sail **g)** cruise **h)** wreck **i)** drown **j)** port **k)** voyage **l)** ferry

1.8.2.5 Raumfahrt

1. **a)** satellite **b)** rocket **c)** astronaut **d)** spacecraft **e)** space flight **f)** space shuttle

1.9 Länder und Völker

1.9.1 *Länder*

1. **a)** Asia **b)** Africa **c)** Europe **d)** Australia **e)** America

2. **a)** United States **b)** Great Britain **c)** Germany **d)** Netherlands **e)** Turkey **f)** Wales **g)** Switzerland **h)** Italy **i)** Hungary **j)** Norway; Denmark; Sweden **k)** China **l)** Belgium **m)** Spain **n)** Greece

3. **a)** The United States is very interesting.
b) We're/We are flying to Switzerland.
c) I come from Scotland.
d) She wants to drive to Poland.
e) We're/We are travelling to Turkey.
f) France is in the European Union.

1.9.2 *Bewohner*

1. **a)** Europeans **b)** Irishman **c)** Frenchmen **d)** Germans **e)** Italian **f)** Dutchwomen **g)** Greek **h)** Chinese **i)** British **j)** Englishwoman **k)** Africans **l)** Japanese **m)** Indian **n)** Dutch **o)** Swiss **p)** Scot

1.9.3 *Sprachen und Nationalitäten*

1. **a)** Swiss **b)** Italian **c)** European **d)** Russian **e)** Austrian **f)** English; Scottish; British **g)** French; Spanish **h)** Greek; Turkish **i)** Portuguese **j)** Japanese **k)** Dutch

ALLGEMEINE BEGRIFFE 2

Zeit 2.1

Jahresablauf 2.1.1

1. **a)** spring **b)** summer **c)** autumn **d)** winter

2. **a)** day **b)** year **c)** week **d)** month **e)** weeks **f)** days **g)** weeks
h) months; days

3. **a)** daily **b)** weekly **c)** monthly **d)** weekdays **e)** weekend
f) season **g)** holiday **h)** New Year's Eve

4. **a)** on **b)** in **c)** at **d)** in **e)** on **f)** in/during **g)** on

Monatsnamen 2.1.2

1. **a)** February **b)** October **c)** July **d)** August **e)** September
f) December **g)** March **h)** April **i)** June **j)** November **k)** May
l) January
January, February, March, April, May, June, July, August, September, October, November, December

Wochentage 2.1.3

1. **a)** Monday **b)** Sunday **c)** Tuesday **d)** Thursday **e)** Friday
f) Saturday **g)** Wednesday

Tageszeit 2.1.4

1. **a)** morning **b)** evening **c)** midnight **d)** afternoon **e)** evening
f) noon **g)** night **h)** morning **i)** evening

Uhrzeit 2.1.5

1. **a)** one o'clock **b)** (a) quarter past four **c)** (a) quarter to three
d) seven minutes past eight **e)** half-past ten **f)** five to two

2. **a)** What time are you coming?
b) I'm coming at three (o'clock).
c) – How long is the film?
– Two hours.
d) You've got/You have thirty seconds.
e) It's six (o'clock).

2.1.6 *Andere Zeitbegriffe*

2.1.6.1 Heute, gestern und morgen

1. **a)** today? **b)** moment! **c)** present **d)** future **e)** ago

2. **a)** past **b)** future **c)** present **d)** present **e)** future **f)** past **g)** present **h)** future **i)** future

3. **a)** during **b)** while **c)** during **d)** while **e)** during

4. **a)** today **b)** Yesterday **c)** Tomorrow **d)** the day after tomorrow **e)** the day before yesterday **f)** days ago **g)** tonight **h)** Last night

5. **a)** date **b)** in **c)** then **d)** Nowadays **e)** When **f)** this **g)** Meanwhile **h)** period

2.1.6.2 Dauer

1. **a)** since **b)** for **c)** since **d)** since **e)** for

2. **a)** while **b)** fortnight **c)** length **d)** for **e)** forever **f)** until/till **g)** still

2.1.6.3 Häufigkeit

1. **a)** – Frequent. **b)** ever **c)** always

2. never, rarely, sometimes, often, always

2.1.6.4 Früher und später

1. **a)** already **b)** soon **c)** at last **d)** on time **e)** first **f)** later **g)** afterwards **h)** after **i)** only **j)** just **k)** before

2. **a)** soon **b)** later **c)** at last **d)** then **e)** only **f)** On time **g)** in time **h)** already **i)** afterwards **j)** late **k)** first **l)** at once **m)** before
n) early

3. **a)** recently **b)** punctual **c)** final **d)** immediately **e)** finally **f)** At first **g)** yet

2.1.7 *Zeitlicher Ablauf*

1. **a)** kept **b)** began **c)** became **d)** went on **e)** got

2. a–w, b–y, c–u, d–z, e–t, f–x, g–v

3. **a)** delay **b)** remain **c)** interrupted **d)** introduction **e)** last **f)** remain **g)** stage **h)** lasted **i)** development **j)** up-to-date

Raum 2.2

Räumliche Begriffe 2.2.1

1. **a)** there **b)** below **c)** lower **d)** far **e)** everywhere **f)** out **g)** narrow **h)** low **i)** left **j)** front **k)** down **l)** under
2. **a)** on **b)** against **c)** over **d)** in front of **e)** behind **f)** next to
3. **a)** deep **b)** side **c)** straight **d)** place **e)** to **f)** Where **g)** opposite **h)** among **i)** flat **j)** distance **k)** room **l)** surface **m)** anywhere **n)** away **o)** at **p)** somewhere
4. **a)** next **b)** nearest **c)** nearest **d)** next **e)** next **f)** nearest
5. **a)** spot. **b)** depth **c)** central **d)** outside **e)** at the top of **f)** at the bottom of **g)** all over

Bewegung und Ruhe 2.2.2

1. **a)** jump **b)** rise **c)** sink **d)** fall **e)** sit **f)** move **g)** turn **h)** lie
2. **a)** rose **b)** raised **c)** risen **d)** lay **e)** lay **f)** lying
3. **a)** house **b)** aircraft **c)** rock **d)** beer **e)** fish **f)** earth **g)** bicycle
4. **a)** balance **b)** floated **c)** shock **d)** slipped **e)** pushed **f)** rise **g)** movement

Schnell und langsam 2.2.3

1. **a)** hurry **b)** overtake **c)** ran **d)** fast **e)** slow **f)** speed **g)** quick **h)** hurry **i)** rushed

Richtung 2.2.4

1. **a)** off **b)** out **c)** along **d)** around **e)** backwards **f)** across **g)** into **h)** towards **i)** through **j)** forward
2. **a)** direction **b)** on **c)** approached **d)** for/to **e)** from **f)** along **g)** off **h)** across

Kommen und Gehen 2.2.5

1. **a)** going **b)** passed **c)** wandering **d)** left **e)** get **f)** appear **g)** Enter **h)** reached **i)** settle **j)** stop **k)** walk **l)** arrived **m)** disappeared **n)** return

2.3 Menge und Maß

2.3.1 *Mengenbegriffe*

1. **a)** dozen **b)** quarter **c)** half **d)** both **e)** few **f)** lot of **g)** little **h)** lot of **i)** many **j)** no **k)** enough **l)** nothing
2. **a)** less **b)** over **c)** another **d)** most **e)** much **f)** few **g)** little **h)** all **i)** least
3. **a)** pile **b)** contents **c)** none **d)** several. **e)** The majority of students

2.3.2 *Grundzahlen*

1. **a)** thirteen **b)** four **c)** six **d)** eighty **e)** forty **f)** twenty-one **g)** five **h)** seventeen **i)** fifteen **j)** fifty-three **k)** forty-four **l)** thirty-six **m)** a/one hundred **n)** twelve **o)** a/one thousand **p)** eleven **q)** nine
2. **a)** six **b)** three **c)** one **d)** fourteen **e)** billion

2.3.3 *Maße und Gewichte*

1. **a)** foot **b)** feet **c)** metre **d)** grams **e)** kilogram **f)** ton/tonne **g)** mile **h)** pint **i)** centimetres **j)** measured; weighed; metres; weight

2.4 Ordnung

2.4.1 *Ordnungsbegriffe*

1. **a)** set **b)** turn **c)** order **d)** quality **e)** arranged **f)** levels **g)** types **h)** rules **i)** series **j)** size **k)** pair of
2. **a)** size **b)** brand **c)** pair **d)** set **e)** kind **f)** class **g)** row **h)** degrees **i)** series **j)** order

2.4.2 *Unterschied und Einteilung*

1. **a)** common **b)** piece **c)** as; as **d)** another **e)** only **f)** same **g)** not a **h)** special **i)** rest **j)** like **k)** alone **l)** especially **m)** next **n)** very much **o)** others **p)** regular **q)** together **r)** besides **s)** than **t)** else **u)** very **v)** different **w)** part **x)** single
2. **a)** combine **b)** separate **c)** limit **d)** include **e)** consist of
3. a–y, b–t, c–z, d–p, e–x, f–w, g–r, h–q, i–u, j–v, k–s
4. **a)** opposite **b)** contrary **c)** normal **d)** typical **e)** usual **f)** ordinary **g)** average **h)** general **i)** main

Ordnungszahlen 2.4.3

1. **a)** 17**th**; seventeenth **b)** 3**rd**; third **c)** 1**st**; first **d)** 1000**th**; thousandth **e)** 2**nd**; second **f)** 4**th**; fourth **g)** 23**rd**; twenty-third
2. **a)** ninetieth **b)** forty-second **c)** hundredth **d)** sixth **e)** twenty-fifth **f)** eighteenth **g)** thirty-third **h)** twenty-first

Ursache und Wirkung 2.5

1. **a)** because **b)** so **c)** As **d)** reason **e)** cause **f)** relationship **g)** therefore **h)** effect **i)** result **j)** due to **k)** condition **l)** In order to **m)** why **n)** origin

Art und Weise 2.6

1. **a)** how **b)** a bit **c)** also **d)** just **e)** all **f)** at least **g)** almost **h)** at all
2. **a)** too. **b)** At least **c)** rather **d)** Besides, **e)** usually **f)** – I do too. **g)** hardly
3. usually, really, even, all, so, mostly, quite
4. **a)** hard **b)** hardly **c)** hardly **d)** hard **e)** hardly
5. way
6. **a)** partly, largely, scarcely, nearly, completely **b)** absolutely, generally, completely, thoroughly **c)** Anyway, Somehow, In any case, Instead, By chance, Otherwise

Farben 2.7

1. **a)** green **b)** black **c)** white **d)** grey **e)** pink **f)** brown **g)** blue **h)** red **i)** yellow

Formen 2.8

1. **a)** cross **b)** knot **c)** corner **d)** circle **e)** arch **f)** line
2.

round	*pointed*
ball	arrow
earth	tip
eye	pin
goldfish bowl	needle
balloon	knife

3 VERSCHIEDENES

3.1 Weitere Verben

1. **a)** burning **b)** dropped **c)** pouring **d)** pricking **e)** stuck **f)** shining **g)** growing **h)** ringing **i)** burst **j)** scratching
2. **a)** belong **b)** hit **c)** handle **d)** introduced **e)** treat **f)** struck **g)** leaning **h)** spare **i)** spread **j)** increased
3. **a)** bed **b)** meet **c)** cake **d)** hair **e)** Goa **f)** poor

3.2 Weitere Adjektive

1. **a)** thin **b)** light **c)** empty **d)** open **e)** off **f)** strong **g)** small **h)** difficult **i)** hot **j)** quiet **k)** old-fashioned
2. **a)** latest **b)** little **c)** big **d)** hot **e)** modern **f)** fat
3. **a)** steady **b)** bright **c)** huge **d)** loose **e)** pure **f)** familiar **g)** ancient **h)** urgent **i)** powerful **j)** stiff **k)** bare **l)** fresh

3.3 Strukturwörter

3.3.1 *Pronomen und Artikel*

1. **a)** Whose **b)** whom **c)** Who **d)** which **e)** These **f)** that **g)** whatever **h)** Whoever **i)** What
2. **a)** her **b)** him **c)** me **d)** us **e)** them **f)** you **g)** mine **h)** theirs **i)** myself **j)** herself **k)** each other **l)** itself **m)** its **n)** yourselves **o)** yourself
3. **a)** somebody; anybody **b)** some; any **c)** something; anything
4. **a)** everybody **b)** nobody **c)** Whoever **d)** such a **e)** No one
5. **a)** Peter is an actor. **b)** The dog has injured its eye. **c)** It was such a nice day. **d)** She had her arms behind her back. **e)** Have you got a better one?

3.3.2 *Hilfsverben*

1. **a)** mustn't **b)** Shall **c)** may **d)** could **e)** could **f)** need **g)** should **h)** ought **i)** would **j)** be able to **k)** mustn't **l)** needn't **m)** might **n)** must

3.3.3 *Weitere Präpositionen, Konjunktionen und Adverbien*

1. **a)** or; and **b)** from;to **c)** about **d)** If **e)** without **f)** for **g)** in; by **h)** as; as **i)** but **j)** that **k)** of **l)** to **m)** between **n)** with **o)** about
2. a–z, b–q, c–v, d–w, e–t, f–y, g–r, h–u, i–s, j–x